supernatural

The Work of Ross Lovegrove

Compassionate Innovation by Paola Antonelli

Reyner Banham, in *Los Angeles: The Architecture of Four Ecologies*,[1] declared that just like the weather, the Hispanic style in the city's architecture was mentioned in conversation only when it was either extraordinarily good or extraordinarily bad but that in truth, just like the weather, it was always there. The same weather-centred paragon, so exquisitely British, could be applied to the relationship between technology and contemporary design. Technology, a fundamental ingredient of design, cannot be switched on and off at whim. In our popular science times, when a paper's technology reports are as keenly perused as its movie reviews, products are often designed to be expressionistic celebrations of new technical possibilities. As if by storm, technology takes over the whole personality of mobile phones and office chairs, rendering objects more complicated rather than simplifying their complexity for our use. It is not difficult to appreciate the enthusiasm that so much progress engenders and the marketing opportunities it creates, but design critics always hope that technology is not the only inspiration behind an object's conception. We seem to want every design to be a sublime synthesis of goals and means. Only a handful of contemporary designers are able to metabolize the most advanced technology until it becomes effortless, so completely assimilated within the project as to seem invisible, only to resurface and deliver subtle surprises as the object is used. Ross Lovegrove, who is addicted to innovation and surrounds himself with samples of weird untested materials, is one such master.

After a brief acquaintance, Ross and I bonded over materials. In 1994, during the preparation of my first exhibition at New York's Museum of Modern Art, 'Mutant Materials in Contemporary Design', I visited Lovegrove's office in gentle Notting Hill, London. The exhibition was based on the idea that technological progress had radically changed the role of materials in the design process. Ross was the perfect champion of the systemic revolution in design that I had in mind. The premise of the exhibition highlighted a new perception of the material world. The period following the end of the Cold War was somewhat similar to the period that followed World War II,

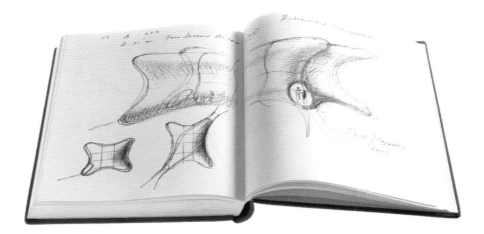

when a fresh injection of previously restricted technologies and new materials contributed to a triumphantly new material culture. Just like the 1950s, the 1990s were optimistic and morally positive times, marked by a renewed attention to domestic living and human mobility, guided by concerns about the environment and a strong international political consciousness, and fuelled by exuberant progress in technological research.

Moreover, new techniques were used to customize, extend and modify the physical properties of materials, and to invent new ones. Materials could at last be transformed by engineers and designers themselves, and adapted in order to achieve their design goals. The term 'mutant materials' was introduced to illustrate this substantial new configuration sparked by the progress in material technology and culture. According to the theory advanced by the exhibition, adherence to the truth of a material, a tenet of historical modern design, was no longer an absolute. Materials had become curiously deceptive and all the while malleable and sensitive to the designer's intentions. Ceramics, for instance, could look and act like metal, just as plastics could feel and perform like ceramics or glass. A hard and monastic-looking wooden stool could be surprisingly soft. A knotted rope could be as sturdy as metal. The new, crafted, high-tech materials not only appeared different from their traditional references, but also had personalities and behaviours that were distinctly novel.

The substances we used to know and recognize have become the basic ingredients for new, displacing recipes, opening up another world of possibilities for designers and manufacturers. No longer adjuncts in passive roles, materials have been transformed into active interpreters of design objectives. Instead of being mere tools in the design process, they inform and guide it. The mutant character of a material is not a mere function of the quantity and diversity of the objects it can produce. It is related to the diversity of behaviours and personalities it can assume. Design is

moved by an endless search for the perfect balance between means – the available materials and techniques – and goals – for example a super-light chair, a mass-produced steel floor lamp, or a new line of low-cost foldable furniture to be sent to disaster areas. In this ancient equation, contemporary materials have acquired an important new purpose, as they are often instrumental in the achievement of even the highest, most abstract, or most general goals: lightness, for example, or recyclability, endurance – even responsibility. With the prospect of a doubling of the world's population by the year 2040, these new priorities and others have become the leitmotif of many celebrated contemporary designers, the obsession of many researchers in materials technology, and a feature of almost instant appeal for consumers.

The multifaceted character of contemporary materials calls for an essentially rigorous and conscious design approach. At the time of the Mutant Materials exhibition, Ross Lovegrove was already leading design's response to this call, conceiving products for a sophisticated public that had learned to recognize patterns of beauty in pragmatic and economic ideas. Unfortunately I had set for myself a limit of no more than two objects per designer, so I chose only a prototype of an elegant plastic razor with a ceramic blade and the Eight chair, which so well represented the new heights achieved by thermoplastics. Over the years, nonetheless, I made sure that I kept abreast of Lovegrove's production, to include some of his new designs in the Museum of Modern Art's collection, and to learn more and more from his work about the essence of contemporary design.

As a matter of fact, the insight that Ross Lovegrove's oeuvre can provide into the new directions of design can carry us much further. To name just two fundamental characteristics, which are not discrete, but rather connected in the designer's material wisdom, Lovegrove's work exemplifies the current importance of crafts and questions the current meaning of 'organic' in design. Crafts first. Contemporary

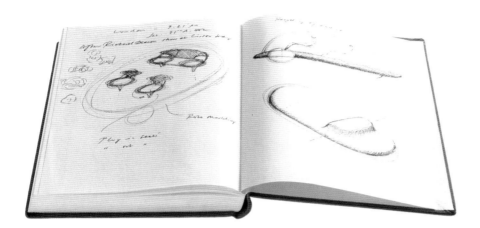

design is a very interesting composition of high and low technologies that offers designers an exhilarating new freedom. In order to master this brave new world, though, an apparently traditional education based on first-hand knowledge of craftsmanship is extremely valuable. As a matter of fact, many advanced materials that can be customized and adapted by designers themselves actually demand manual intervention because the tools to work them do not yet exist and have to be designed, too. England is historically the country where craftsmanship and engineering have shared the most productive dialogue and Ross Lovegrove, who was born in Wales but studied at Manchester Polytechnic and at the Royal College of Art in London, is equally at ease with new alloys as he is with wicker, as demonstrated by his fine chaise for Driade. His passion for engineering has also found fertile ground in the country where structural engineering has forever been considered a branch of aesthetics.

In the 1980s, Ross's temporary stay in Germany, where Frogdesign hired him fresh from university, acquainted him with the needs and possibilities of real industrial production. At Frog, Ross worked on Sony Walkman products and on Apple computers, among other projects, and started developing his own personal, un-Teutonic and sensual approach to product design. He then spent time in France, where his innovative design style fitted well with that of peers such as Philippe Starck and Jean Nouvel. In 1988, back in London, he set off on his own and was finally able to modulate his personal design language.

From the start, his language was labelled 'organic' in quick appreciation of its curvaceous appeal. Ross Lovegrove's design is indeed organic, but its organic nature does not stop at the surface. Nature has forever been an inspiration for architects, engineers and designers. Long before Leonardo da Vinci and Buckminster Fuller, humans all over the world imitated forms that already existed in nature as optimal responses to functional needs, as well as symbolic ones. Organic design is a

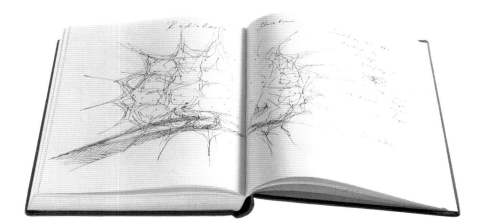

natural choice. Yet, as Peter Reed writes in his introduction to *Objects of Design*:2 'In modern design, there is no single idea of nature. Nature is a cultural construct whose meanings are as varied as its forms.' Today, designers view nature not only as a repository of comfortably humane forms, but rather as a sensible and sustainable system that provides answers to several fundamental questions concerning industrial production.

Contemporary organic design mirrors not only the shapes, but also the structural solutions and efficient systems found in nature. While it is immediately recognizable in the curvilinear forms made possible by the use of the computer in design and manufacturing and applied to all scales of production, it is at other times subtler, hidden in the function, performance or lifecycle of the object. It comes alive for instance in the exceptional brilliance of new pigments in street signs, the vividness of some advanced computer screens, or the fluid responsiveness of some diving fins. In Lovegrove's work, it can also be read in the thoughtfulness that is devoted to each single project, in the economy of thought and logical beauty that pervade the design process, and in the rotundity not only of the object, but also of its lifecycle. It shows, if one can attribute this virtue to design, compassion towards typologies of objects, materials and functions. There is no compassion without curiosity, the need to know more about other people and spheres. This is perhaps the essence of contemporary organic design: reaching out, beyond the traditional limits of one's discipline, in order to learn how to contribute fully and organically to the future of the world.

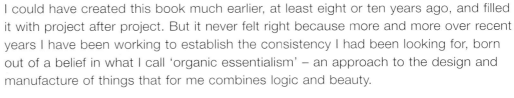

I could have created this book much earlier, at least eight or ten years ago, and filled it with project after project. But it never felt right because more and more over recent years I have been working to establish the consistency I had been looking for, born out of a belief in what I call 'organic essentialism' – an approach to the design and manufacture of things that for me combines logic and beauty.

I have, over the last two or three years, been taking deep breaths to pause and reflect on the design profession, its motivations, its meaning and its future relevance. In these years I have read and written more than I had ever done previously, quite instinctively, and have actively spent time with visionaries in other fields such as engineering, transportation and architecture. This was undertaken with a view to understanding how boundaries begin to overlap and blur in the creation of a rich and exotic new physical environment that is representative of the twenty-first century and reflects the enriching potential of our increasing technological capability.

This book therefore comes at a time of reflection. Its purpose is to lay out the various interests I have and to express the creative freedom and diversity that I have always been drawn towards, remaining open to possibility and change, not locked into any programme.

I have felt a growing interest in what I do from people in fields other than industrial design, who want to share knowledge and work from a point of collective potential, inspired perhaps by some of the principles that are articulated in this book. This moment therefore is one of speculation and adaptation for me – a new millennium, a new studio, a new outlook and perhaps a future in design that remains experimental and intuitive, free and always open in spirit to new possibilities. I feel there are opportunities to contribute progressive and optimistic ideas to fields that have far-reaching global and cultural impact, such as the future of transportation, urbanism and the sensual quality of our physical environment.

process

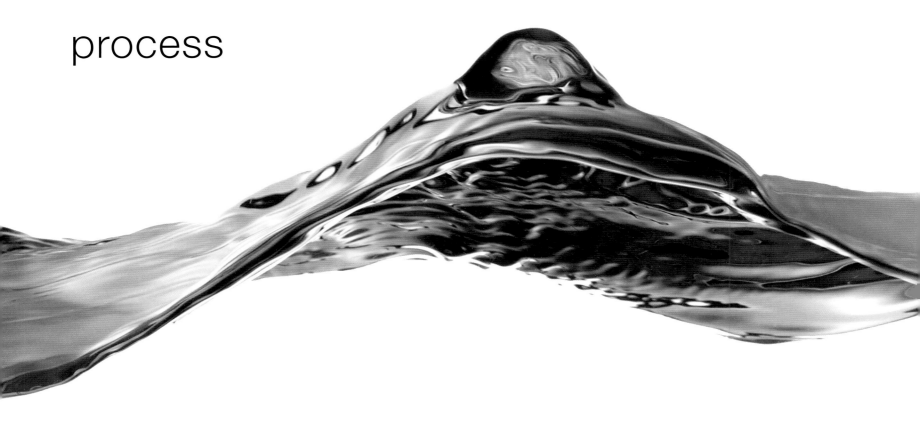

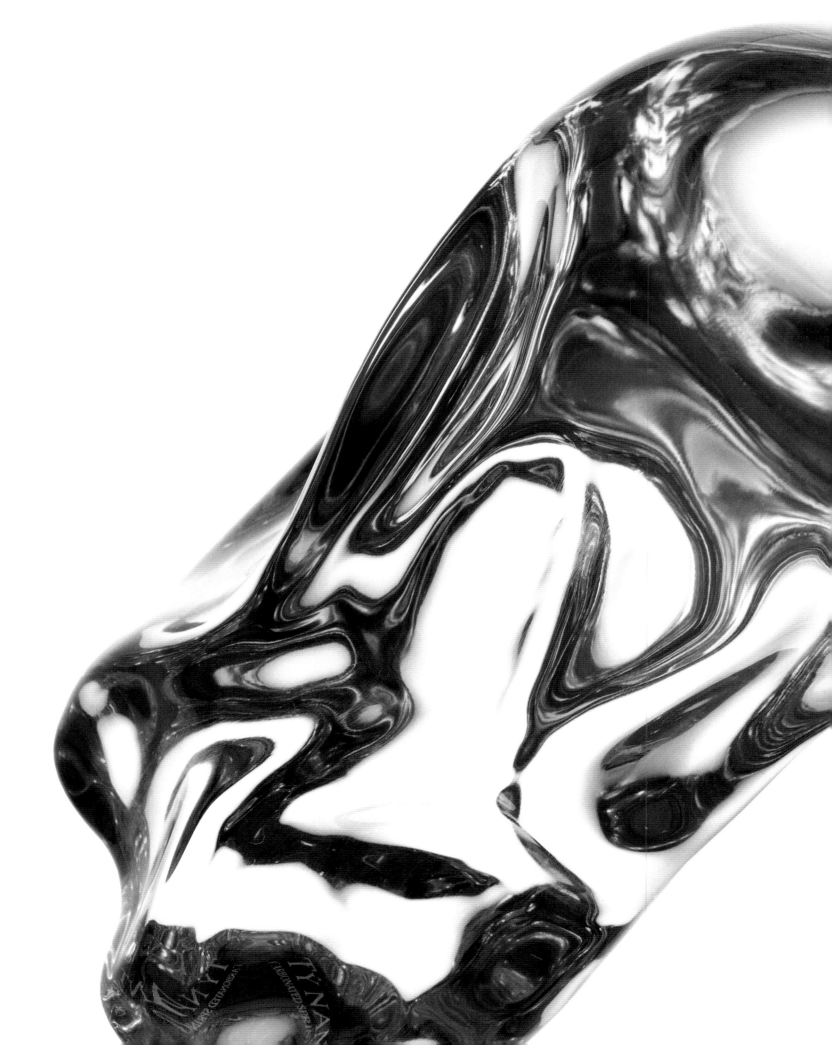

Ty Nant Waterbottle

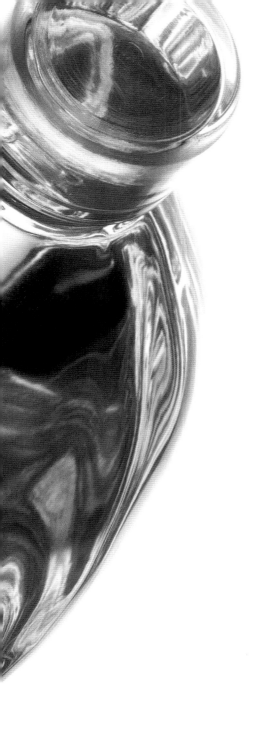

I have a non-linear mind that is stimulated by the rare and the layered. I assemble ideas from a seemingly unrelated plethora of sources that gel into being over time when the moment is right for a concept to materialize. I have few preconceptions and respond to circumstance. Indeed whatever environment and whatever culture I am in at the time will totally affect my perception of modernity, physicality and creativity.

Awareness and accumulated experiences help me to open up new routes that may never have been taken before, based on my own personal understanding and speculation as to why something has, should or could exist for whatever reason – usefulness, aesthetic beauty, or ideally the inherent coexistence of both.

I allow myself to remain receptive at all times to possibility and influence, constantly documenting ideas and thoughts which remain as seeds that might later be cultivated in a conscious or subconscious way in my work. In this way I have resisted the need for a systematic method, preferring to pre-edit my thoughts through notebooks. These allow me to retain any important information and help me create a dialogue with myself. This practice occurs long before I share these thoughts with others.

If you look at my notebooks you will find that they are more like diaries, in that they document the hopes and anxieties in my life at a particular time. They are therefore not only an honest account of the working out of compositions for everyday products and furniture, but they also display liberated freeform conceptualizing on broader issues, such as cars and the construction of new forms in architecture. I need to see things in the round, in three dimensions, with perspective and shadows irrespective of scale or material. This is because most of my design is centred on the individual singular object that remains unattached to its environment.

My character dictates that I constantly live within a swirl of emotions and misgivings that lead me to question right down to the bone the very need for things.

By contrast, on a good day when a clear path is formed, I can envisage a three-dimensional object with such optical precision in my mind's eye that it seems to me to already exist. This constant imbalance between the utopian and dystopian is what colours my thinking with a sense of what is right or wrong, banal or visionary, possible or impossible. These questions are directly related to my conscience as an industrial designer and my sense of the inevitable, in that what man thinks often becomes a reality, as part of our evolving life on this planet.

I use whatever tools are at hand to visualize and communicate these ideas, from simple foam architectural models to sophisticated computer programs, rapid prototyping and the use of samples[1] to prove to a manufacturer that what I am proposing can be realized. Much depends on whether I am in my studio or away travelling, since when travelling the ideas have to be accurately transmitted via digital means. This can often lead to unexpectedly good results, as the method of communication forces one to be more direct and economical.

I have a very clear and precise view of the 'objective' I wish to achieve, and the work begins once this process gets under way. My ideas necessarily flow through countless people, from studio assistants to client engineers, all of whom see things differently and often without the same purpose, motivation or sense of value; they all need reassurance and guidance, in order to support, supplement and achieve a meaningful result. We have to understand that the process of design in itself is a form of education for improvement.

Defining new enriched solutions requires constant reanalysis and cross-referencing through conversation, debate and re-education. I acquire this through literature and spending time with people who stimulate in me a continued awareness of innovation at a more scientific, cross-fertilized, human-centric level.

My resulting work is thus made possible by a shared vision with the manufacturer or patron, who often come to me for the value of my approach and for my

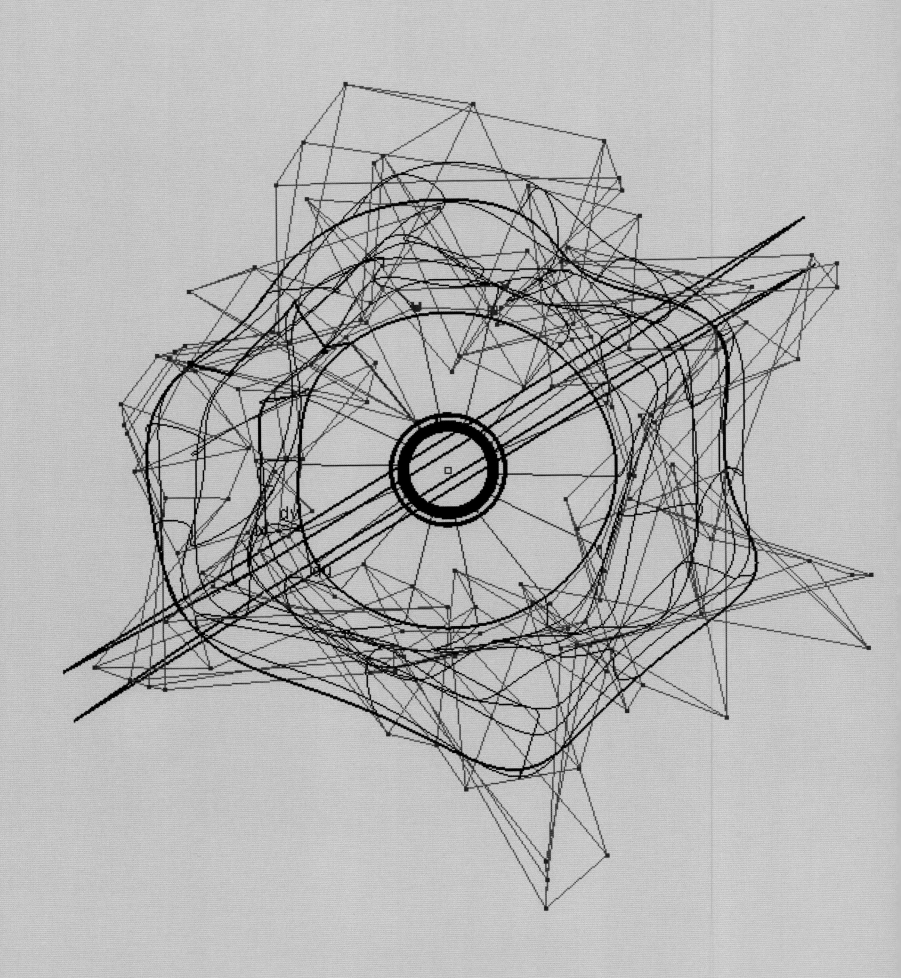

understanding of how to create something culturally and commercially concise. More often than not, I utilize the same processes, materials and technologies that are there for others to create from.

My search for an aesthetic consistency as a reflection of modernity is very important to me in all that I do. I have great admiration for those designers who manage to retain this consistency whilst working across a vast field of typologies, technologies and cultures. Their aesthetic is formed by their particular belief and conviction in what they do and by their ability to communicate the core value of this commitment and passion.

We all have different approaches and objectives as designers. Who can really say what is good or bad, relevant or irrelevant, when the beauty of life is the great diversity of possibility and the incredible momentum of creativity that is enriching all fields. I for one need a foundation for my design that I believe in as something relevant, questioning and progressive. This is something that I feel I can express to others with an underlying logic that does not undermine the intelligence of people who view the world through thinking eyes.

1   I often use reference material of existing industrialized objects to validate the feasibility of my ideas or to act as an iconographic marker for my physical objectives. These contemporary samples supplement the need to rely on the imagination of others and help traverse the multicultural and global nature of my professional field. A good example of this technological and ideological transfer, that feels natural to my instinctive process, are the coated swimming goggles. They are being used to communicate the future surfacing capabilities of my Goggle Light for Luceplan and my Skincare Packaging for Issey Miyake, currently in progress, where a surface coating such as this has been proposed to protect the cream from the ageing properties of UV light.

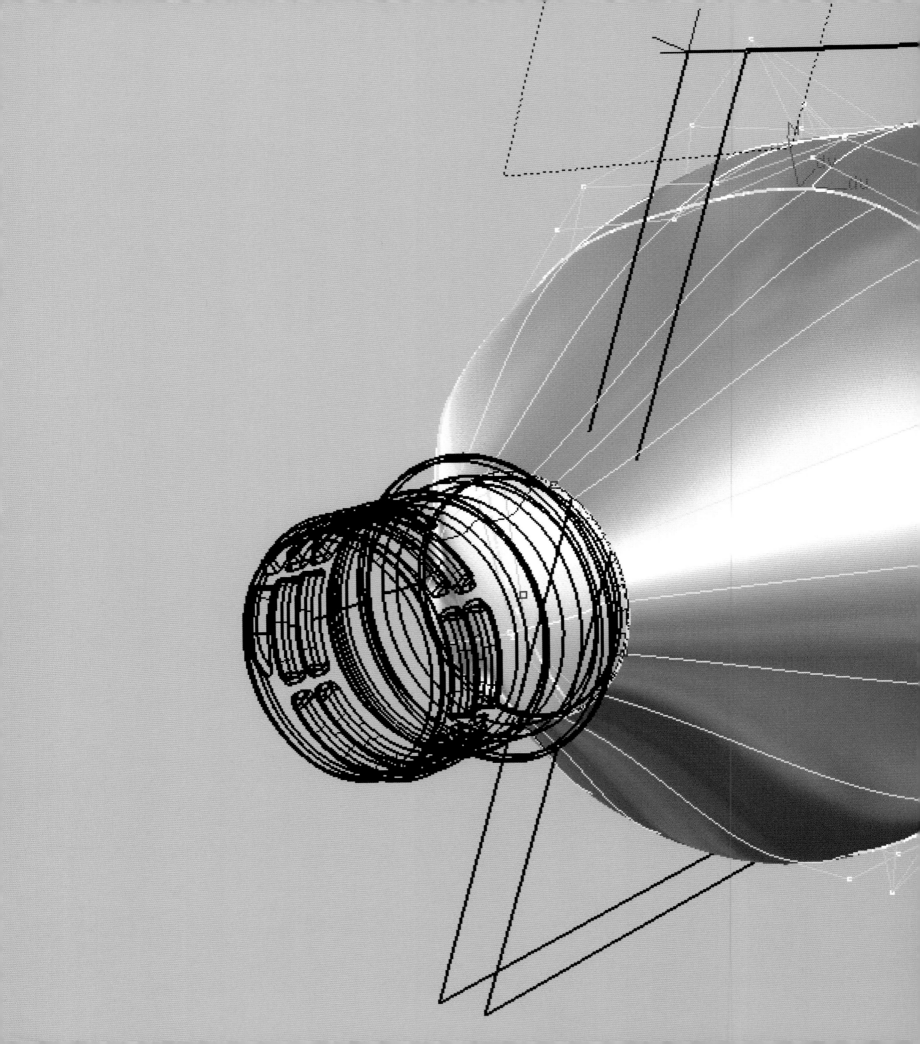

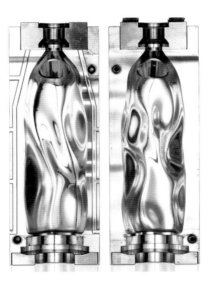

Ty Nant Waterbottle Production Tool

This single production tool was produced to make an initial run to test the quality of the liaison between the two halves and the appearance of the non-linear part line on the blown bottle shape.

It was machined from aluminium and further 'production' tools were made as six bottle-forms in three sizes of 50, 100 and 150 cl in separate blocks to provide the necessary production volumes.

Ty Nant Waterbottle Study Model

This study model has been machined from the data acquired from the scanning and refinement of the surfaces of the initial foam sculptures. It is made from solid acrylic and was used to demonstrate the optical qualities that could be achieved when a transparent PET vessel is filled with pure filtered water.

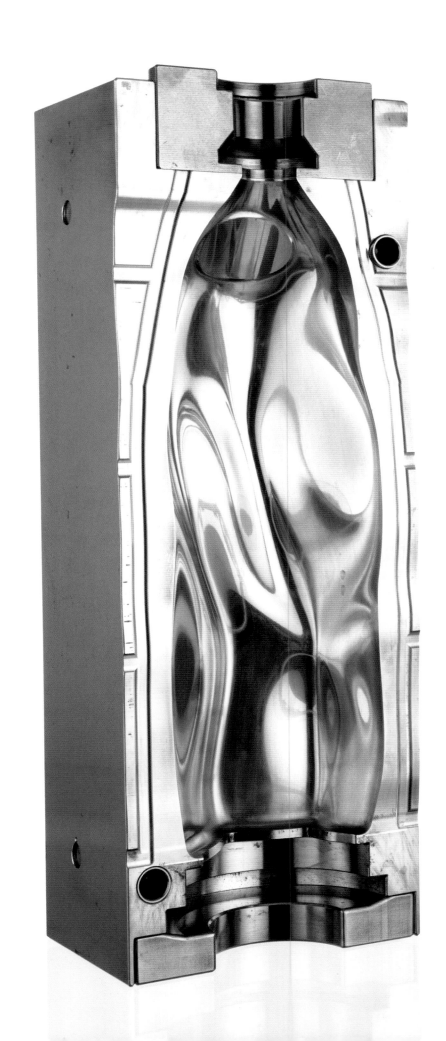

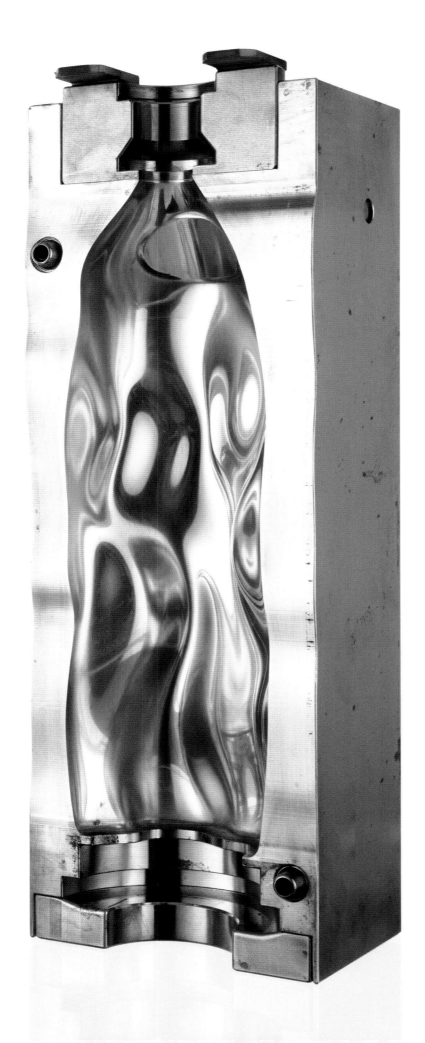

Water Form by Tokujin Yoshioka

The name of Ross Lovegrove is now synonymous with organic design. It is a misunderstanding if one simply considers him to be the distinguished designer of beautiful soft curves and organic shapes, since it is not soft curves that characterize his design method. For Ross Lovegrove, soft curves are of little significance. What is most important is his knowledge of and research into the interactive relationship between humanity, nature and technology. Every possible factor and its inevitabilities are carefully taken into account and reflected in his designs. Those soft curves, therefore, are the result of his signature attitude towards design.

The greatness of his design lies not only in its essential feature of beautiful curves and lines, but above all in the various underlying emotional aspects of his products.

At the very first sight of the plastic waterbottle for Ty Nant, I caught my breath at its design. It appeared as if brimming with generosity and spontaneous beauty, freely arisen from the world of design. I still remember the startling moment when I learned that Ross Lovegrove was the creator of the bottle and realized that everyday consumer products like plastic water bottles could be transformed into such a charming art through Ross's dialogue and interaction with objects. As if Ross Lovegrove casts a spell over the raw material, the thin plastic and the mass of water finally creates a sculpture of light and shadow.

When setting out to design a waterbottle, 'form' and 'shape' are never the objectives. The essence of Lovegrove's ideal waterbottle design may be found in his high respect for the incomparable, eternal beauty of water, and great knowledge and appreciation of things that exist in nature. The direct expression and passionate delivery of water was the result of his approach to designing the waterbottle. It seems, therefore, that his aesthetics and appreciation for organic forms and lines are condensed in this single object.

Regardless of the fact that the bottle is an everyday consumer product, it is a masterpiece whose poetic and sensual elements reveal it to be a signature Ross Lovegrove design.

The plastic waterbottle design perhaps symbolizes the humanity of Ross Lovegrove himself who, since our first encounter in Milan in the spring of 1998, has always exuded warmhearted exuberance as generous and honest as nature itself.

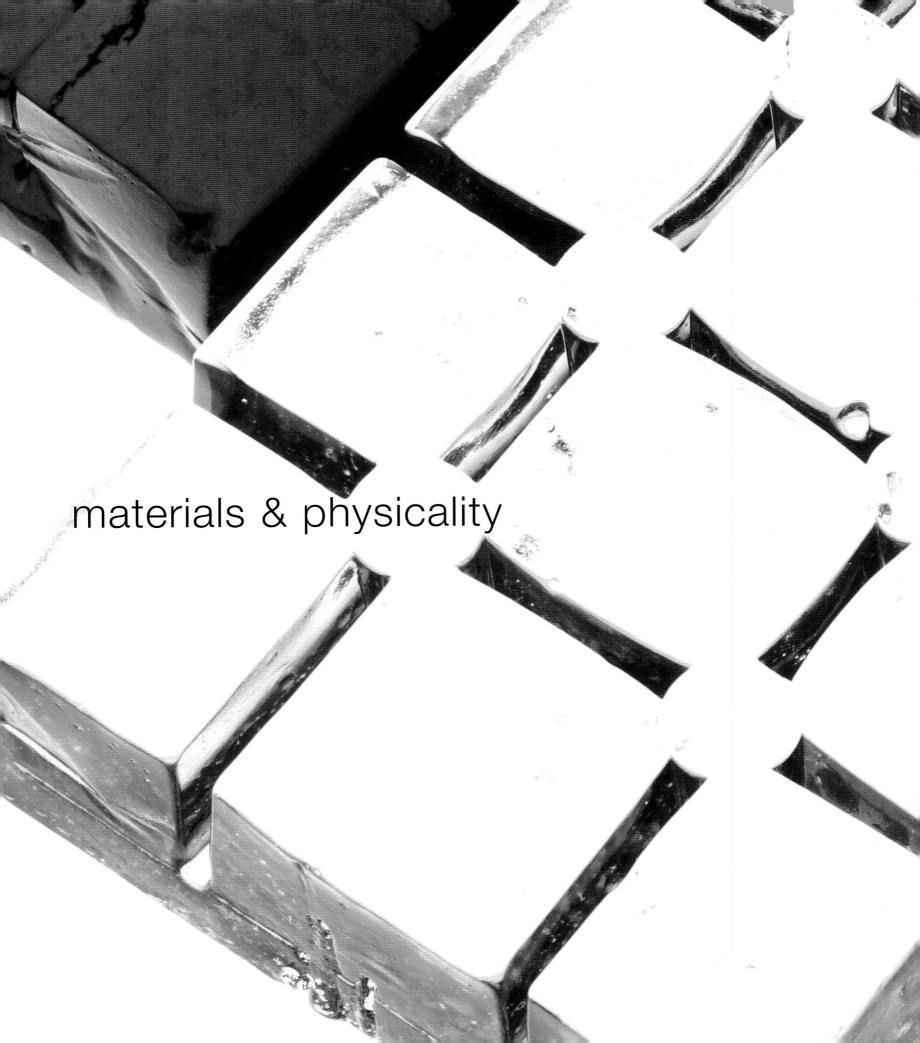

materials & physicality

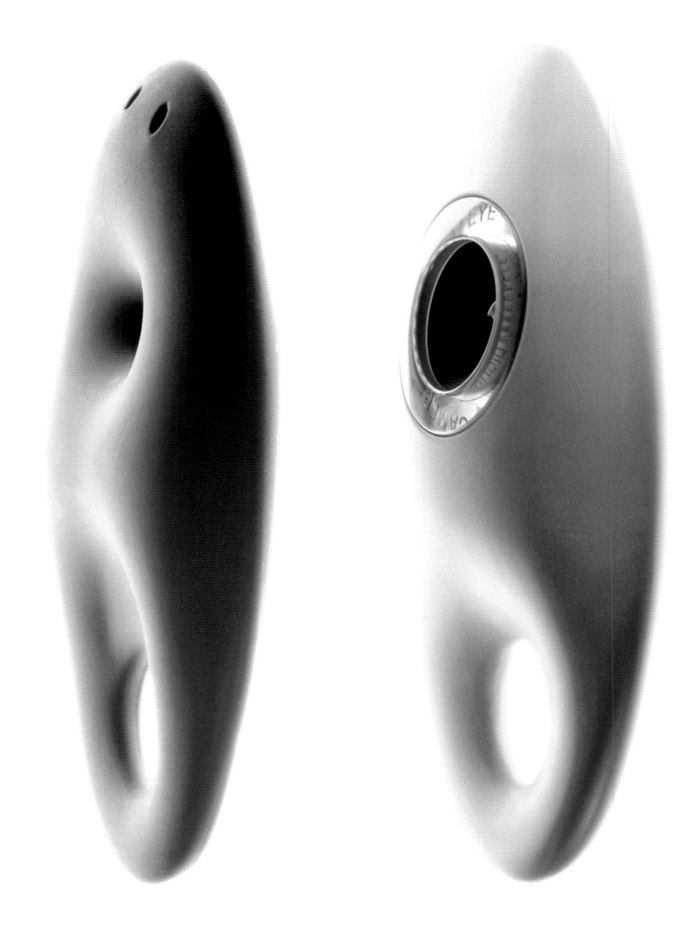

Domestic Science

I have always had an instinctive understanding of materials. This is something within my subconscious that very much conditions my reactions to things made, or conceived as ready to be made. Therefore, as an initial reaction, I often sense things rather than analyse them. And my designs, which emanate from this first feeling, frequently display a balance that is often diluted in designs that are laboured over and subject to too many external voices.

My first understanding of this was as a child. I was brought up at a time when everything it seemed was beginning to be subjected to processing, industrialization and polymerization – from food and its packaging through to home furnishings and clothing. We were becoming more and more detached from the source or origin of products, and natural materials were being replaced by the synthetic or man-made.

Yet even then, I never felt that this in itself was a negative factor because with such mass industrialization, a resourcefulness and economy can be achieved, making things go further and creating the most from the least. As a family the economics of our situation meant that everything was reused, reheated or recycled, imbuing in me a resourcefulness and a deep sense of appreciation for things. This emergent synthetic condition felt modern and progressive, bringing with it a new physicality in colour, texture and composition that, being alien, was stimulating and in its own way quite liberating.

In fact I knew no different, since this was the world I came from. And so later, when I began to study domestic science, or cooking, at school, my approach to discovering the physical limits of food was shaped by the organic tactility of materials in their raw state and their subsequent transformation through heat into substances which seemed so radically different from what they had originally been. This transformation of state so fascinated me that I broke all the culinary rules, more preoccupied with the blending and blurring of seemingly incompatible substances, in

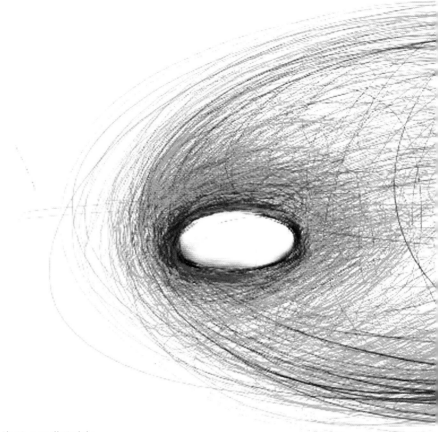

search of something with new physical properties rather than those that predictably emerged from a cook book.

For example, I was amazed at how a single substance, such as an egg or a potato, could be manipulated to achieve such unique and often contradictory structures, densities and forms. If one thinks about this phenomenon it is truly remarkable that the origin of most industrial processes can be traced to or paralleled in the way organic matter changes state through the physics of cooking. Here I first discovered foams, suspensions, elastomers, crystalline structures, honeycomb and fibrous materials, solids that became liquid then reverted to solid again and powders that, when combined with dairy products and sugars, could become rock hard, only to disperse again in water.

Today, as I read about the concept of bio-mimicry and its premise of emulating the phenomena of the natural world, very little surprises me as I know from my childhood experiences that remarkable new structures can be conceived through direct observation of and experimentation with biodegradable compounds.

Transparency, Softness and Lightness: Three Illustrations

Over the years, as part of my approach to manufacturing, I have been drawn towards proposing a new physicality in products, one that combines structural and aesthetic innovation. In many respects these proposals were only original in that they were conceived via the cross-transfer of material technologies from one field to another. Observation of this nature has always played an instinctive role in my approach to design. Indeed today, as the blurring of boundaries between creative disciplines is leading the way forward into new aesthetic territories, the concept of cross-fertilizing materials and technologies is becoming the rule rather than the exception in the quest for innovative solutions.

The Basic Thermos Flask, first conceived in 1987, explored the relationship between the inside and outside of a product, conveying in its transparency an honesty of

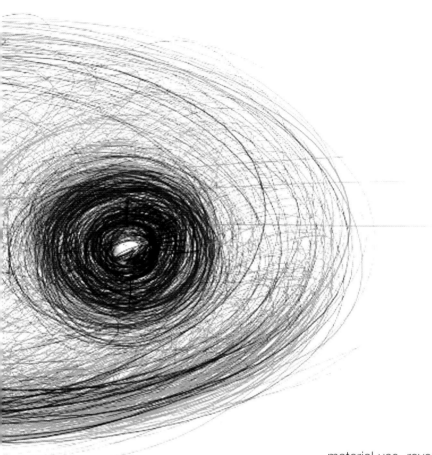

material use, revealing its true composition without effect or pretence. Its optical nature reduces its mass whilst retaining an essential geometry to provide a harmony between its form, function and material. It has been designed for disassembly and in such a way that the assembled product is not compromised by losing any of its inherent completeness even if the connection details between components remain apparent. Such composition, made possible by material application and precision manufacture, creates products of a higher value than simply their material or functional content.

I see a relevance in such a system for the future manufacture of cars, whereby revealing their contents will only highlight their preciousness – that is, both technology and man.

'A design may be called organic when there is an harmonious connection of the parts within the whole, according to structure, material and purpose. Within this definition, there can be no vain ornamentation or superfluity, but the part of beauty is none the less great ... in ideal choice of material, in visual refinement and in the rational elegance of things intended for use.'[3] Eliot Noyes

Later, in 1992, I entered into the study of digital cameras, an emergent technology without a clear typographical position at that time. I was fascinated by this since a decade earlier I had recognized whilst experimenting with disc film formatting at the Royal College of Art that new technologies gave rise to new typologies. These required grounding in their lineage in order to be related to people's simple understanding of essential functions.

The resulting Eye Camera concept – which I went on to propose to the Olympus Optical Company in Japan – housed its parts within a hydro-elastically formed body that was soft and anatomical, mimicking the way our own bodies are made as a combination of hard and soft materials for great performance and resilience. This approach was influenced by the early studies of Mario Bellini for Olivetti into membrane surfaces for integrated computer terminals and, most notably, his remarkable Divisumma adding

'Through the familiarity and understanding of formal and tactile relationships, we acquire an appreciation of the invention of nature and man – hence any change in the emotional climate of our environment becomes a matter of artistic consideration.'[4]
Isamu Noguchi

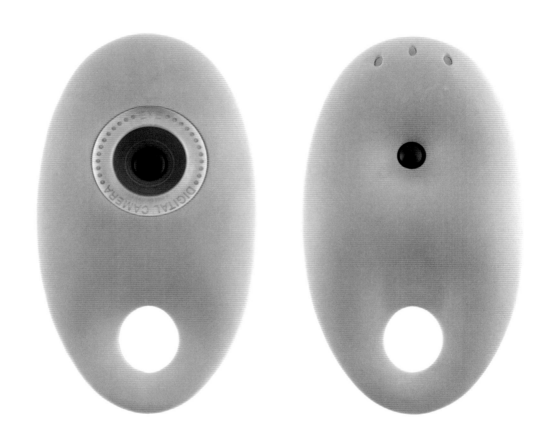

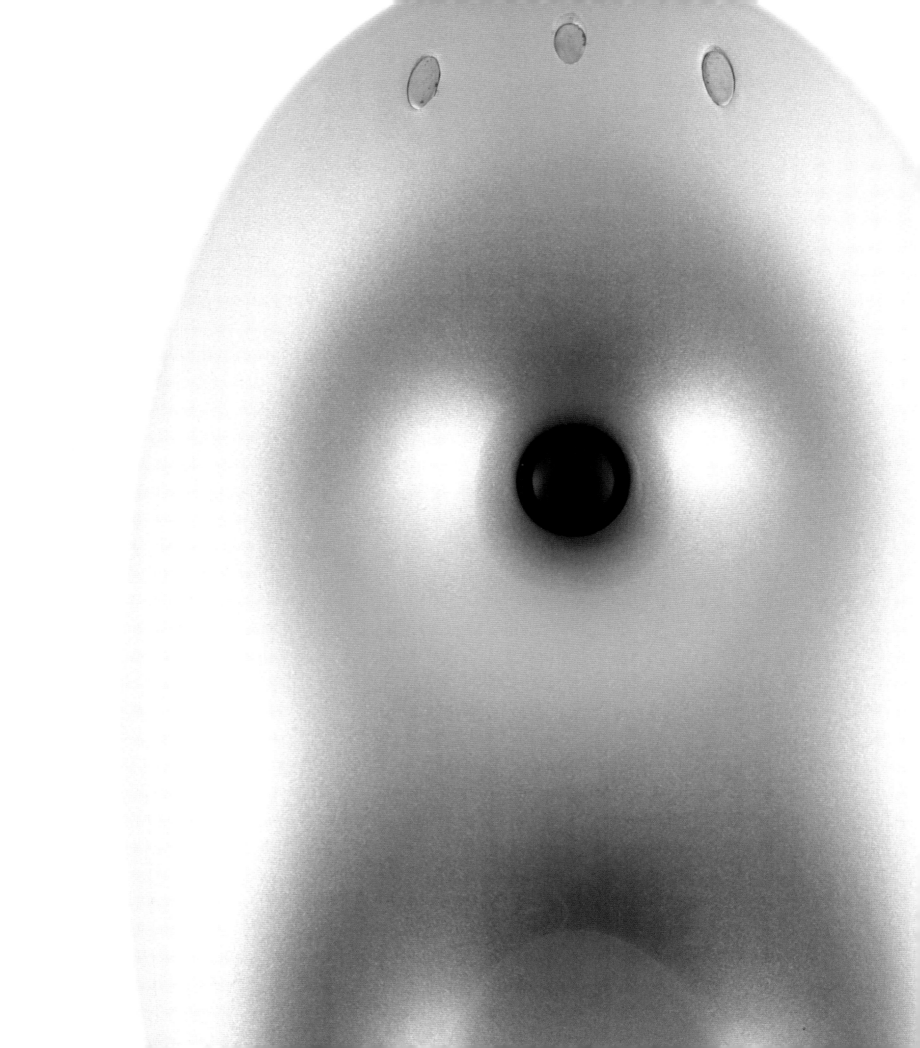

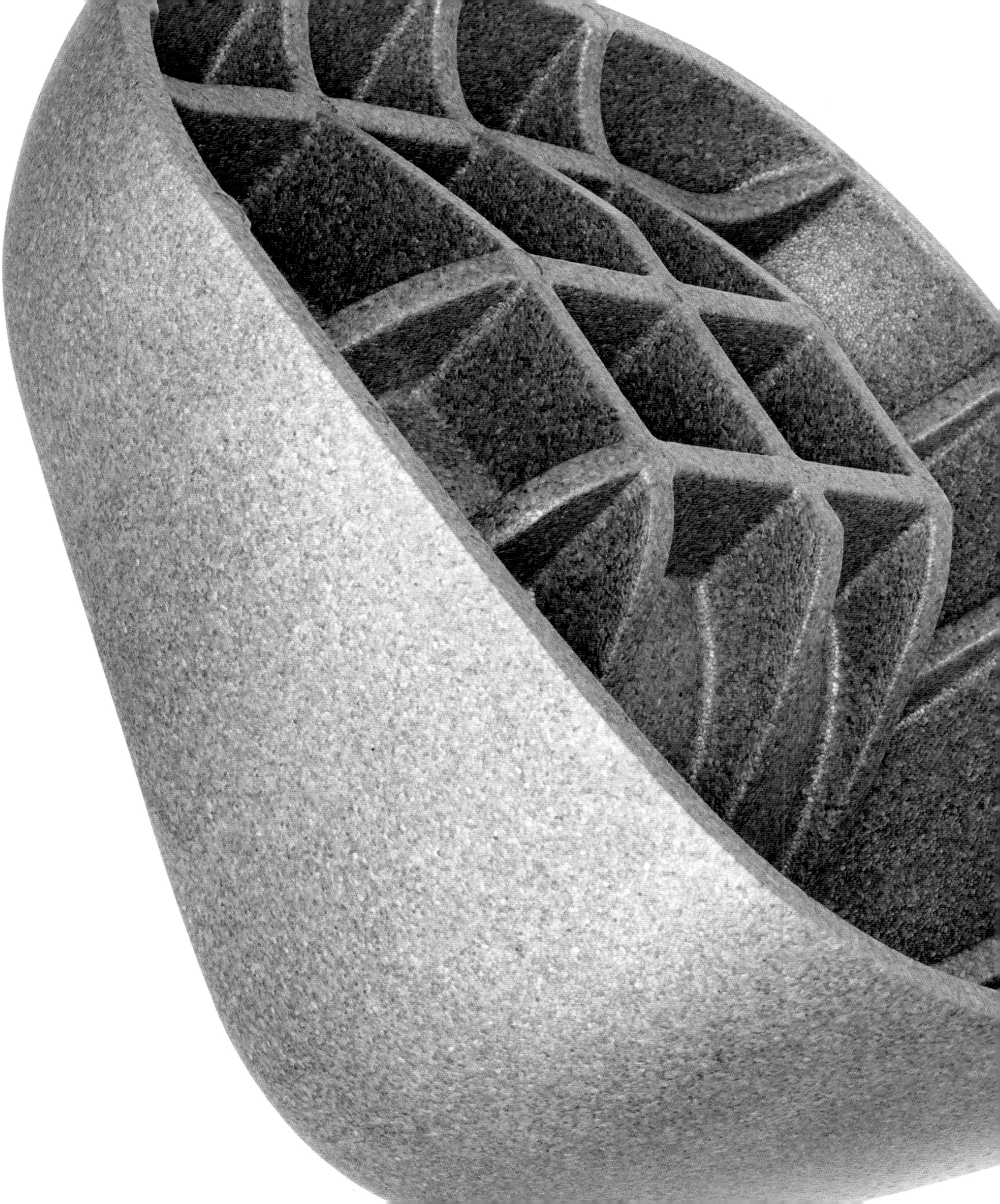

machine. This had been designed in 1973 and embodied a new aesthetic that was holistic and thoroughly progressive in its fluid architecture.

As a nomadic object the camera assumes a role that is almost prosthetic in relation to the user, meaning that its physicality is both intuitive and sensual. Its materiality therefore came about as a natural consequence of its non-precious existence as a dynamic tool for living. With data now recorded digitally without moving parts, the opportunity arose to mould an impermeable skin about an inner circuit board. Its form was developed by membrane moulding between the essential external points of human interface such as the lens and recording button located under its surface.

It was thus not so much designed as evolved with the feel of a biological organism that grows from intrinsic and extrinsic forces, rather than being mechanically constructed. Today this approach and its resulting aesthetic purpose remains as something that continues to inspire me. I wish to create products that are only made possible by the technology of the times in which we live, thereby helping to enrich our perception of modernity and progress.

My third illustration of material appropriation is that of the Air One and Air Two seating pieces for Edra in Milan. This armchair and stool were conceived out of a long and adventurous relationship with PP (polypropylene), beginning ten years before with Knoll in the USA and their Surf collection of computer accessories.

My lifelong interest in packaging, its lightness and the perceived value of materials were the impetus behind such a project, for I was always aware that the so-called 'transient materials' we throw away can have value in their own right, if indeed a valued application can be found. I find it quite obscene to discard the PP foam packaging of a computer, television or white goods because they are often beautifully designed and functionally vital with layered properties. They can be rigid yet forgiving, warm and tactile, insulatory and resilient, lightweight, economical and recyclable, properties derived with purpose from high physics and polymer science.

There is an incredible potential in the future for foams as we strive for lightness in architecture, products and transportation. However, we need to understand better the potential of polymers and carbons in manufacturing to create flexibility in form production and, with it, inherently purposeful structural expression.

'Lighter materials ... these happen to be the organic ones: polymers and composites. They are simply lighter because their main building stones are the lighter atoms: hydrogen, nitrogen, oxygen and carbon and they can be composed into materials of great strength.' [5] Adriaan Beukers

If one pieces all this together, the concept of lightweight, stackable, portable furniture springs to mind quite naturally as a popular application. The Air One Armchair formed part of the interior installation of the Serpentine Summer Pavilion in London, designed by Toyo Ito in 2002. It philosophically connects with the architecture by extending the theme of structure and material research into the seating. It plays with permanence, impermanence, the expression of light and lightness in mixed-medium environments.

At present I am engaged in the study of modular architectural systems from this particular polymer foam's material and manufacturing technology in order to arrive at

structures that are not burdened by the need to support their own body-weight, and that inherently make good use of the thermal, acoustic and weather-resistant characteristics of this unique low-density polymer.

I also continue to work on PP foam development on a direct human scale with Rolf Fehlbaum at Vitra. We are trying to make the technology more accessible as furniture for children and schools, at a price commensurate with its informality whilst retaining the charm of the material's non-precious origins.

Thoughts on Future Manufacture and Resulting Physicality
In speculating how the future use of material resources and their application will map out, I can see a path emerging in manufacturing that will split into two arteries. Two quite distinct species of physicality will be created that will impact on our environment.

Firstly the path of precision manufacture and the hyper-refined will continue on as before. A new surface quality will be generated that will see glass run seamlessly into transparent polymer then into aluminium as economic 'single skin' architecture and transportation. This physicality will be born out of the use of highly refined materials that are virgin in their purity, and the resulting aesthetic will reflect this superclean holistic approach. They will remain pristine because with the demise of fossil fuels, and their replacement by new, clean energy sources we will eliminate the carbon particle pollution that coats our cities with such primitive effect.

In parallel and in direct contrast to this path will be the emergence of 'craftech', the creation of manufactured components and products that are made from more experimental processes and material combinations. We will see grasses mixed with polymers to create organic composites that will appear fibrous and earthy. We will also see the development of materials that are wholeheartedly the result of mimicking processes in the natural world where the genetic combination of polysaccharides and proteins create remarkable structures that are resilient, enduring and yet break down organically in water.

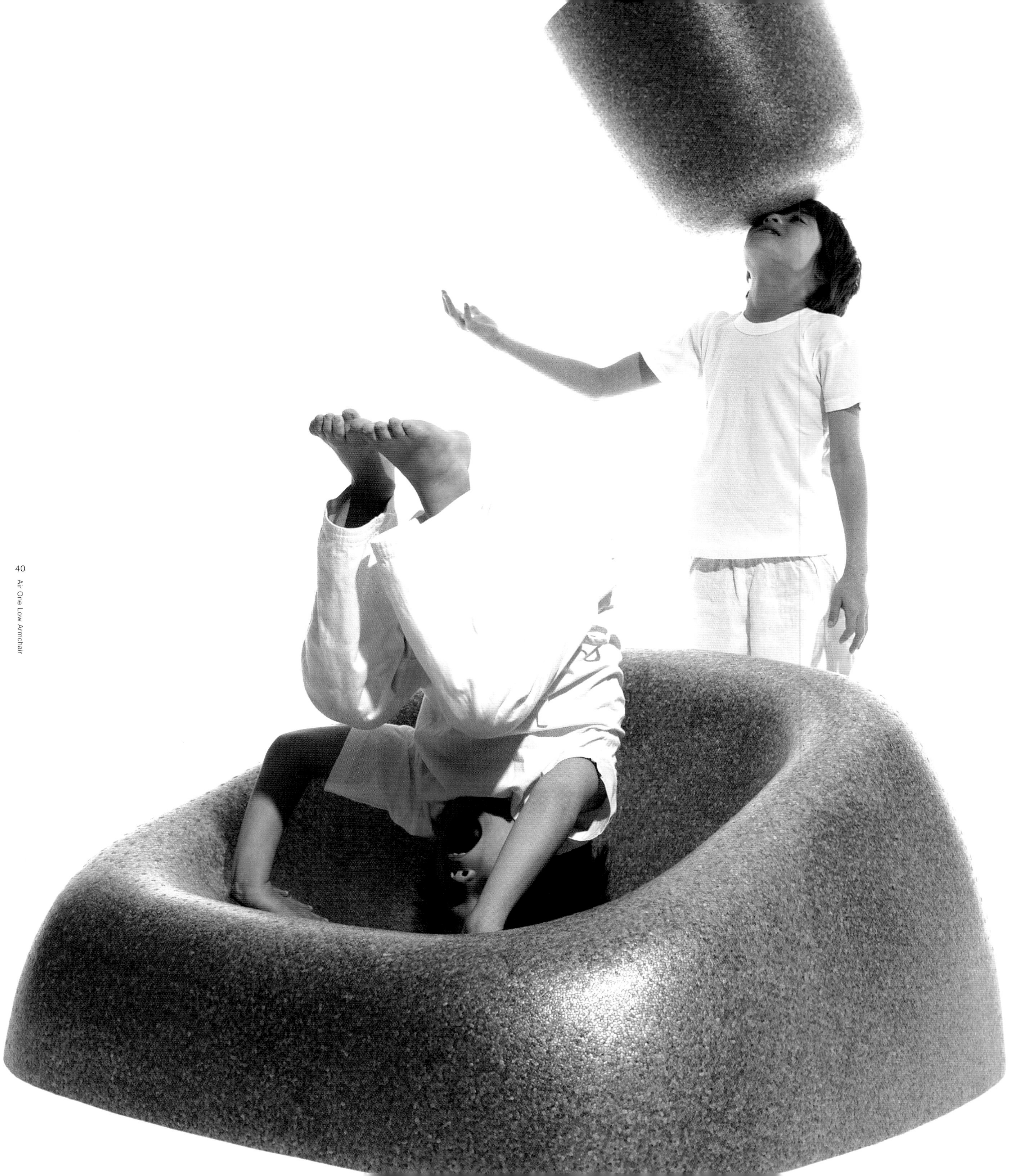

'Biological catalysts also allow nature to manufacture benignly; instead of using high heats and harsh chemicals to create or break bonds, nature manufactures at room temperature and in water. The physics of falling together and falling apart – the natural drive toward self-assembly – does all the work.'[6] Janine M Benyus

This is a new science that will question our current understanding of beauty in the manufacture of industrial objects since the resulting materiality will not convey precision or perfection as we currently know it. Ironically these materials will be more advanced and high-tech but to many of us, the perception of them will be the opposite of what we expect modernity to be. We will therefore need to find ways to communicate a new value system in accordance with the new fibrous composite aesthetic that will emerge.

These new products will appear as rigid textiles and the beauty will strike us in the complexity of intricate surfaces, their composite matrixing and a richness of depth created as materials are grown, interwoven and fused in unexpected combinations. The products to be born out of this approach will be created as much out of ecological necessity as out of a new view of engineering and physics.

We will need to extrapolate the most from the least, and so the blending of grasses like hemp or bamboo – which grow prolifically in nature – with synthetic fibres and recycled polymers is an instinctive and inevitable path. It is sure to generate an unexpected beauty that will reflect our biological relationship with nature.

'A pricing scheme that ignored environmental costs was a silent perpetuator of [pollution, and the degradation of the environment]. Because the economy put no price tag on resource drawdowns or on pollution, it gave no incentive to extract sustainably, process cleanly, or optimize use.'[7] Janine M Benyus

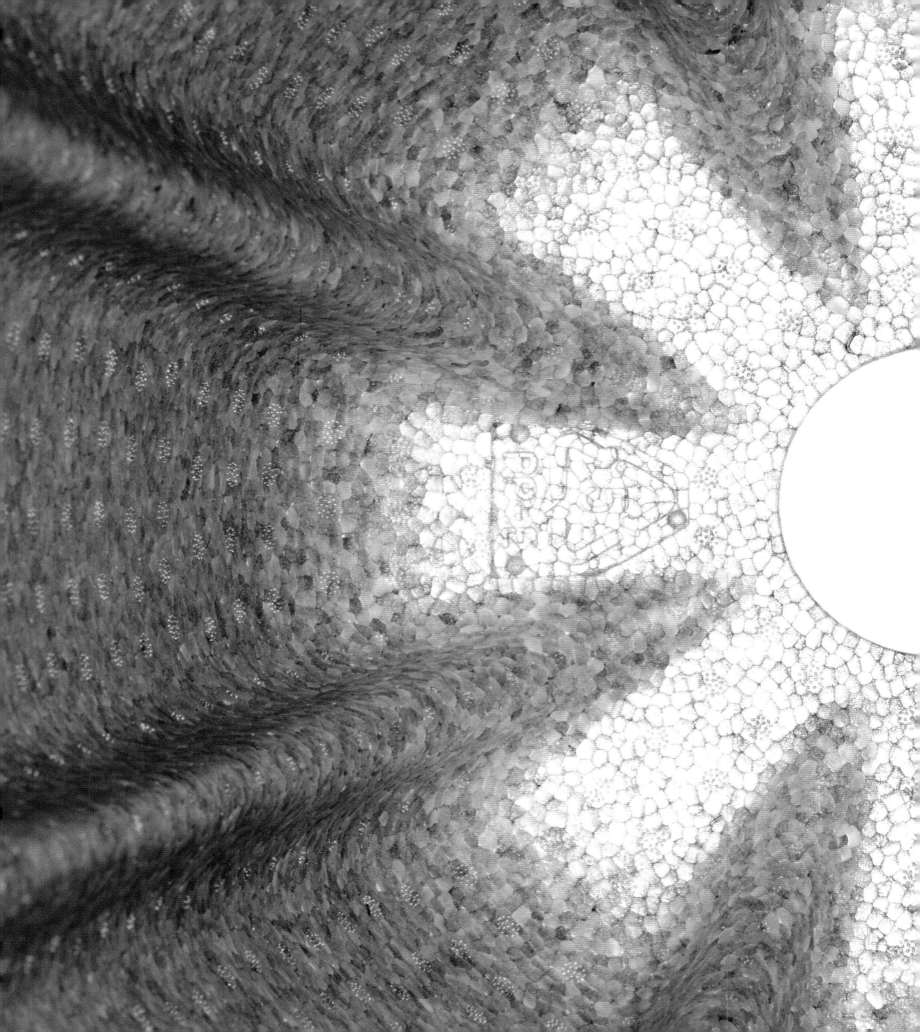

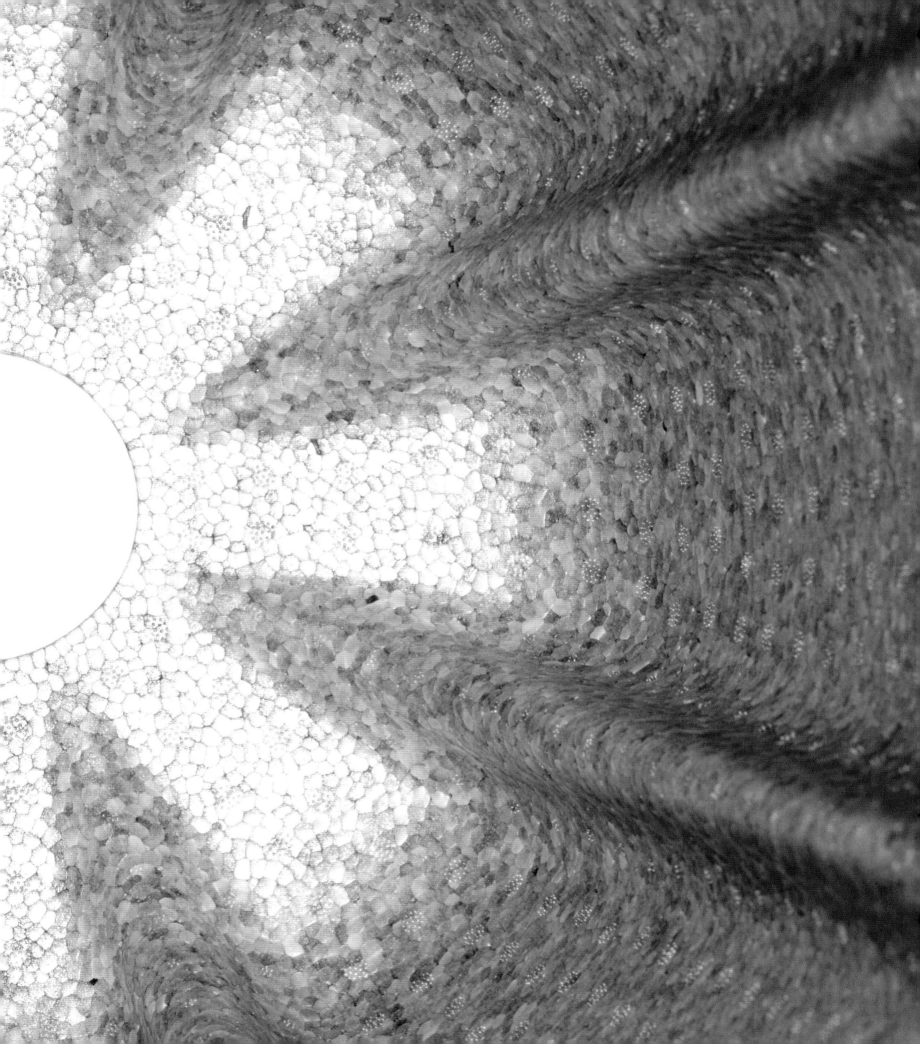

Basic Thermos Flask

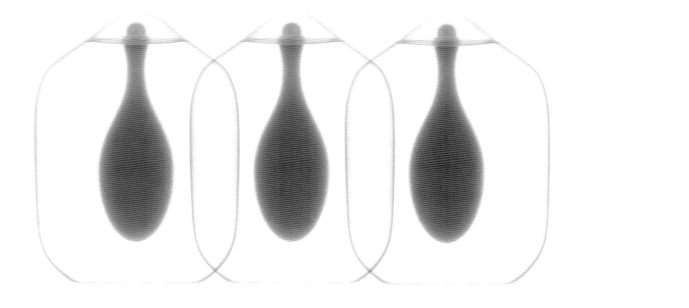

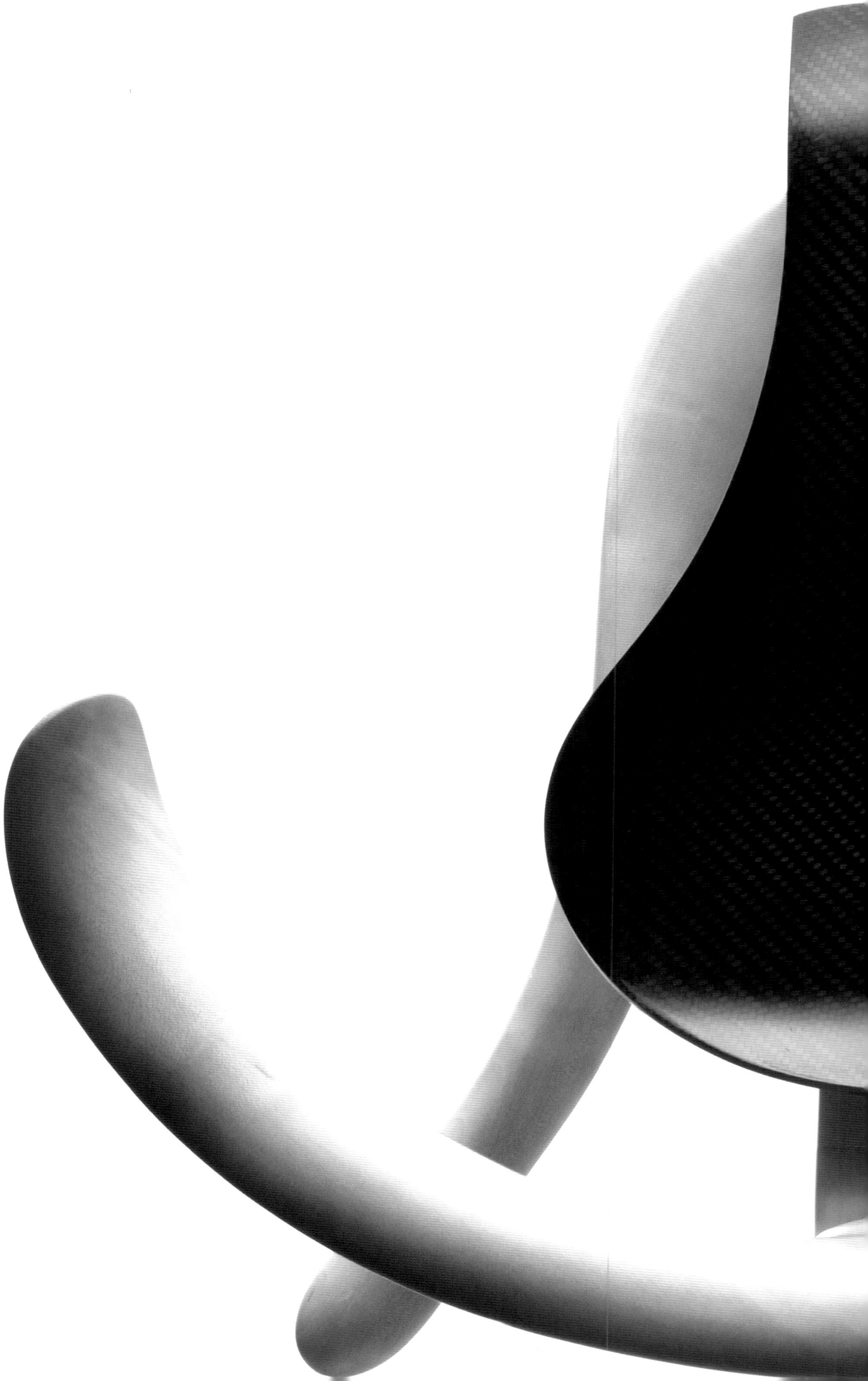

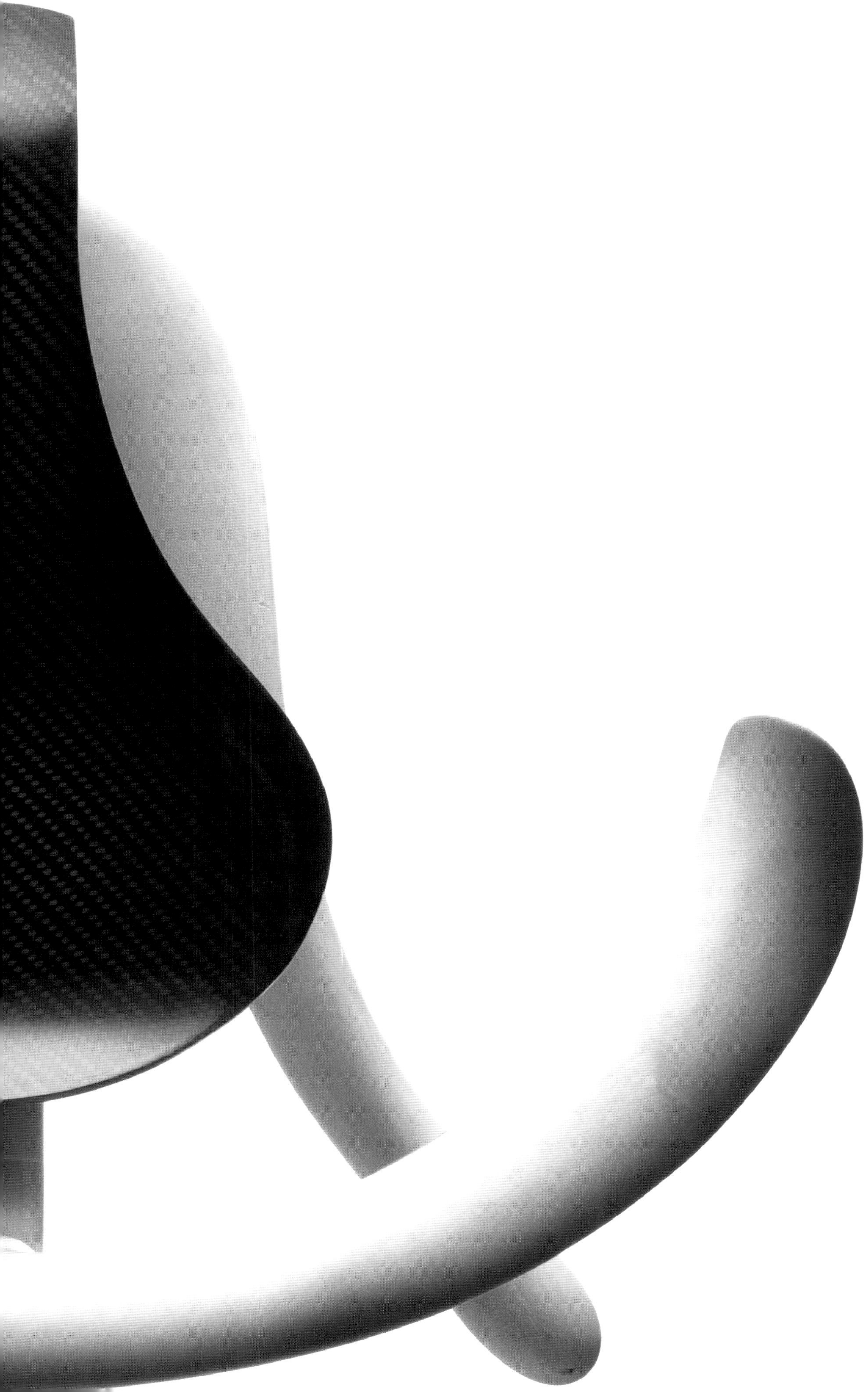

Wooden Shoes
Unknown origin, probably Tuareg,
North Africa

Purchased on Portobello Market in
1998. The evidence of wear around
the toe area represents the reverse
process of design whereby erosion
through use can describe the truth of
form inherent in the object and the
beauty that originates from it.

Wooden Headrest
Ethiopian origin

Purchased from Owen Hargreaves on Portobello Market in 1999, the piece as a block has been sculpted to produce the most from the minimum of operations.

It communicates with abstraction but without ambiguity its purpose even when detached by time or distance.

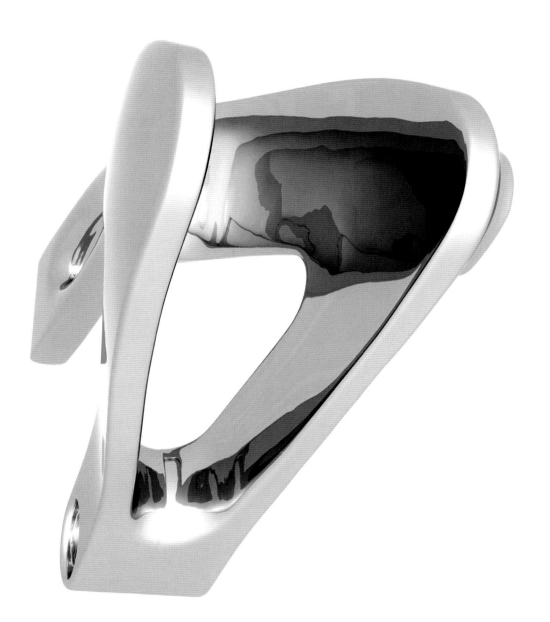

**Biolove Aluminium Bicycle
Superformed Frame**

The superform process in aluminium is
a contemporary method of making
low production runs of components
mainly used by the transportation
industry.
The frame as rendered here on Alias
software describes the three-piece
construction and the intended duality
of finish; matt anodized on its outside
surface and mirror polished on the
inside of the wishbone to create
reflections that are a result of the rear
wheels, rotation adding a form of
optical safety device.

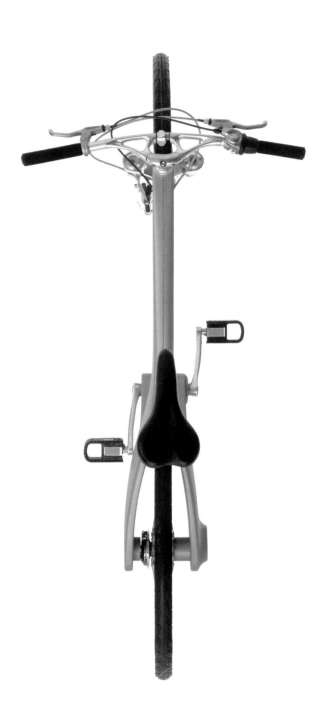

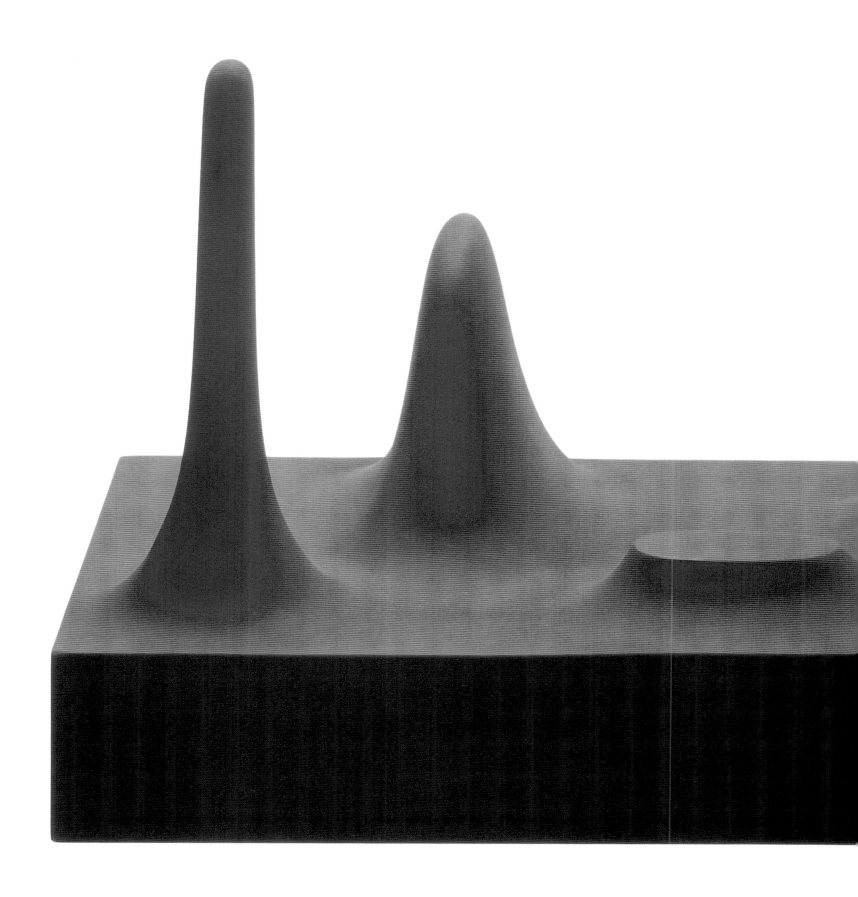

Public Seating Concept Study

This fifth-scale model was an initial study into the ergonomic layout of the seating's functional configuration related to social use. It describes a topography that is elevated from a single monoblock to create abstracted forms for seat backs and table surfaces.

Six models were made; firstly an initial studio sculpture was made in painted white foam, then one gloss black (the master mould) followed by five cast pieces, one red, one mirror, one translucent and finally one photoluminescent model that was given as a gift to Giulio Cappellini in 2001.

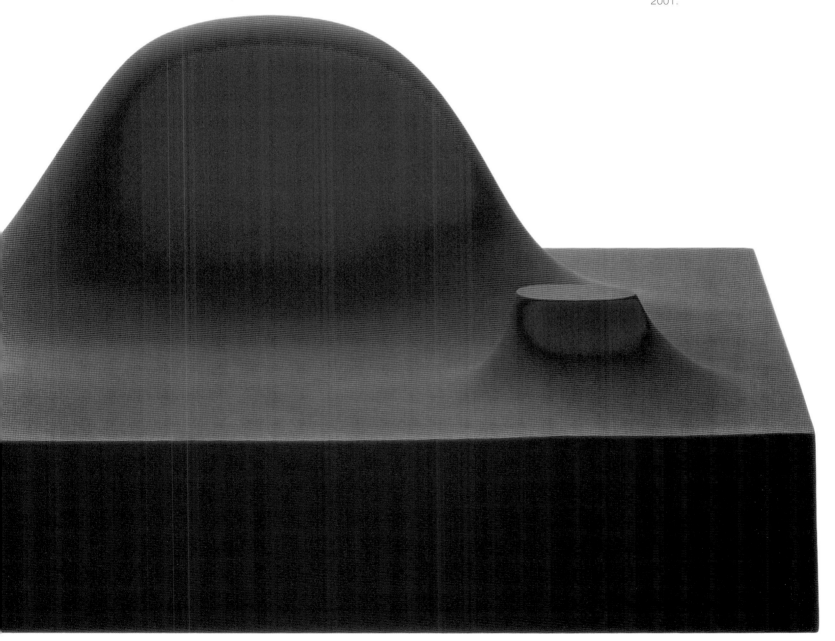

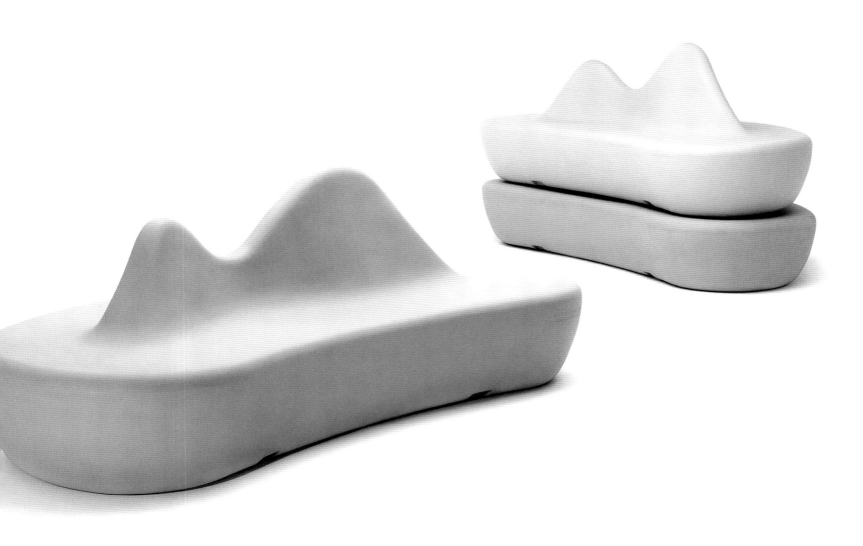

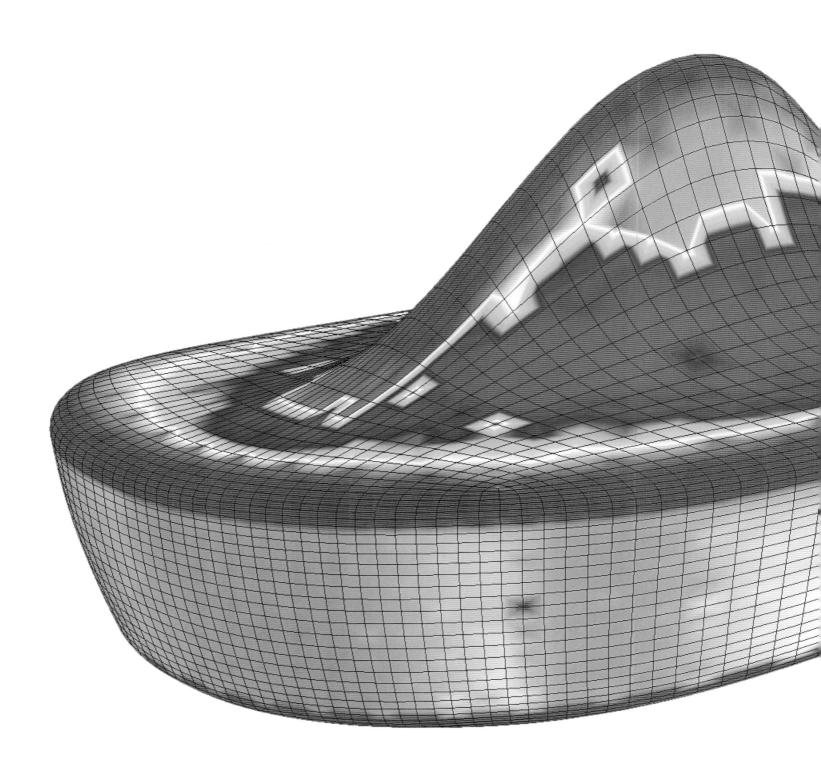

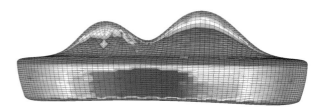

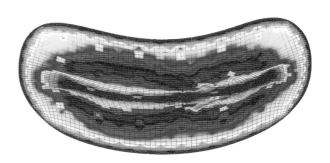

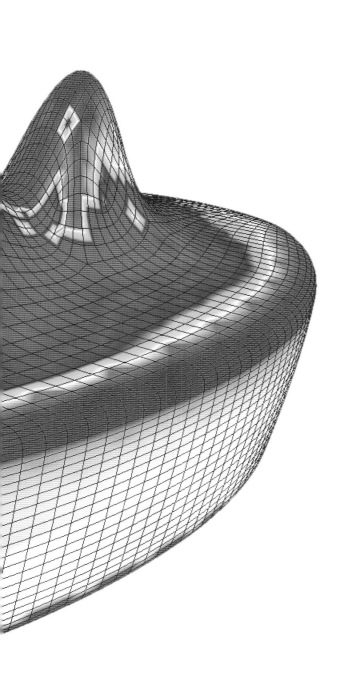

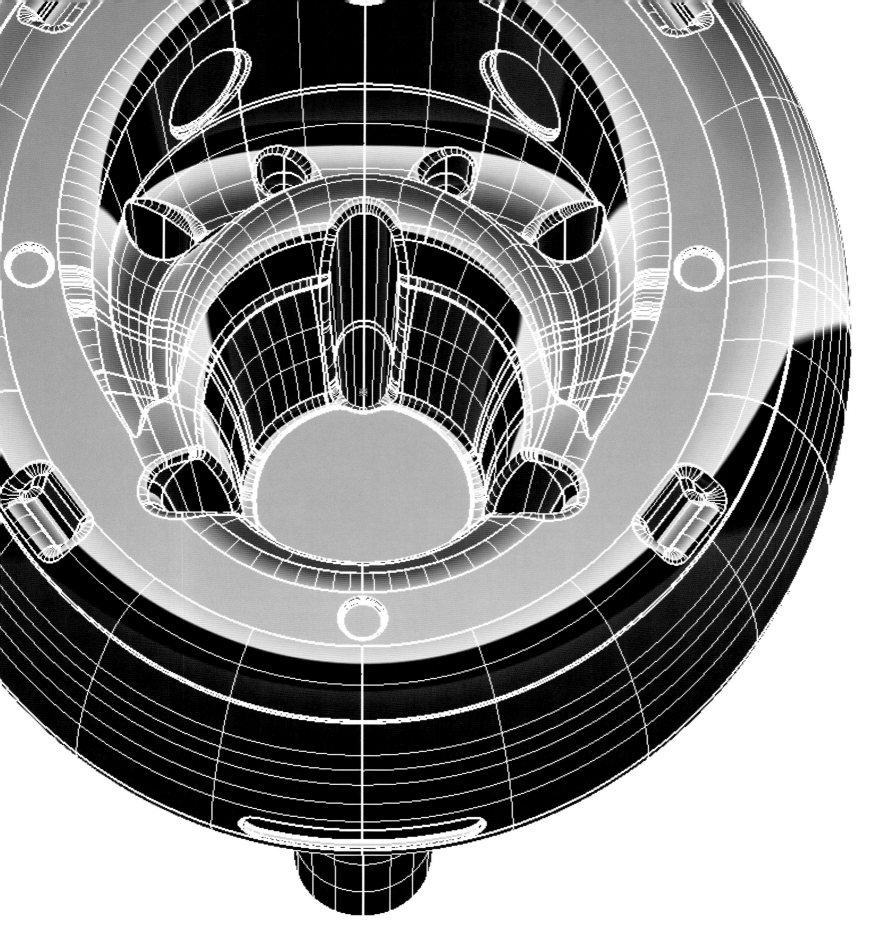

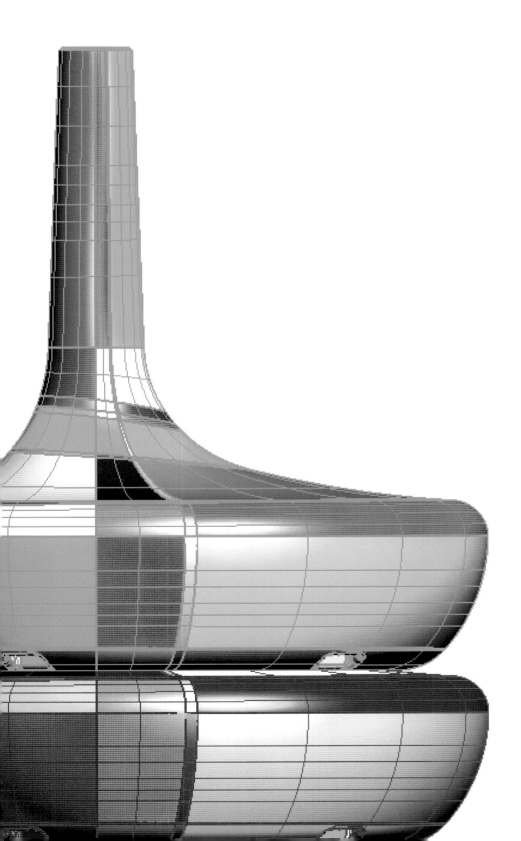

structure & technology

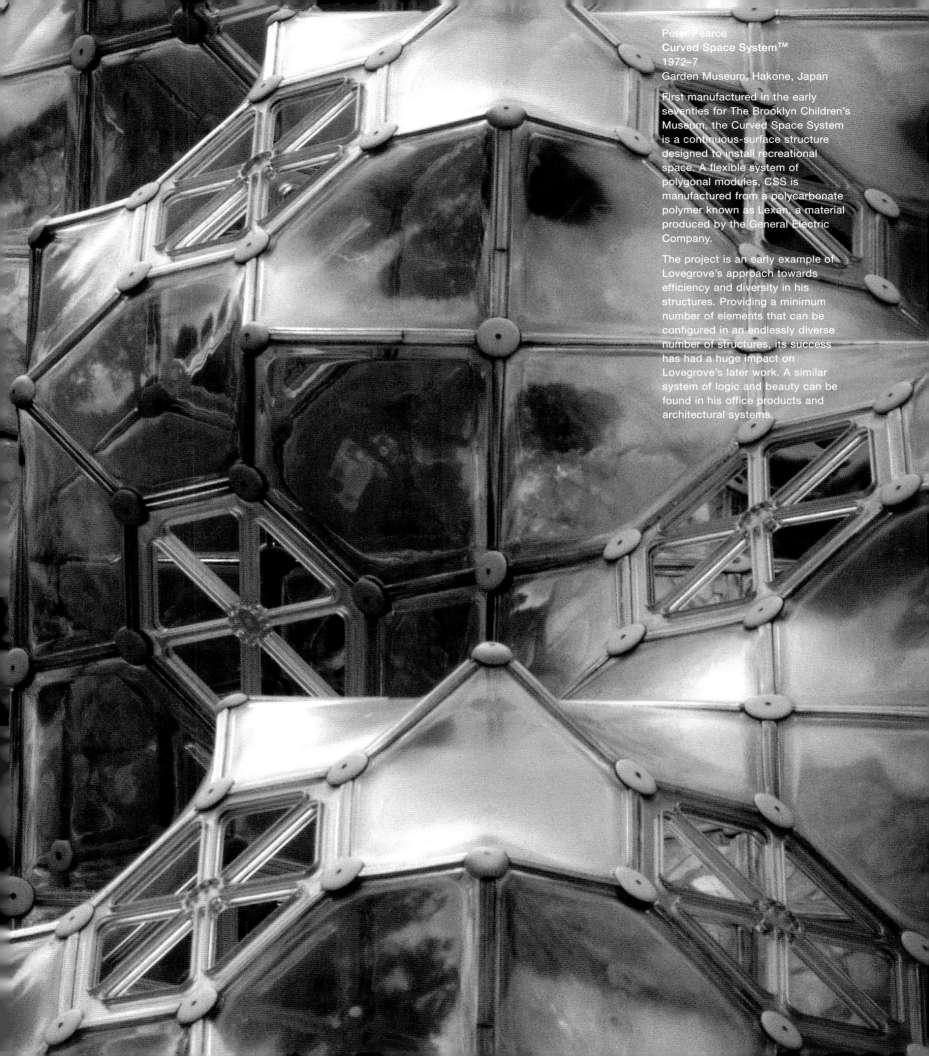

Peter Pearce
Curved Space System™
1972–7
Garden Museum, Hakone, Japan

First manufactured in the early seventies for The Brooklyn Children's Museum, the Curved Space System is a continuous-surface structure designed to install recreational space. A flexible system of polygonal modules, CSS is manufactured from a polycarbonate polymer known as Lexan, a material produced by the General Electric Company.

The project is an early example of Lovegrove's approach towards efficiency and diversity in his structures. Providing a minimum number of elements that can be configured in an endlessly diverse number of structures, its success has had a huge impact on Lovegrove's later work. A similar system of logic and beauty can be found in his office products and architectural systems.

In 1995 I was approached by Herman Miller in the USA to consider the concept of an integrated office environment. My proposal examined how a new relationship could be formed between man, modern materials technology and the way that power and data can flow uninterruptedly through architectural environments. This project, undertaken over a period of five years, introduced me to the concept of minimum inventory, maximum diversity systems and their relevance to the manufacture of office systems furniture. This is a field of manufacture that by definition is high volume, high investment; it is dependent on advanced materials technologies and the application of state-of-the-art production principles to reduce cost and provide the most versatile level of system adaptation from the least number of component types. The design of such an efficient system is a mathematical and logistical puzzle that is based on the notion that there should be no surplus as a result of its modularity and that all parts can relate and reconfigure with ease and intuition. My objective with this system was to facilitate a paradigm shift in the way that space is organized in relation to linear architectural principles, establishing a discipline that would in fact liberate the ultimate physicality of the collective environment away from density and towards lightness and translucency.

All space is united via a single surface, the floor. It seemed logical therefore to exploit this fact by designing a raised tile matrix that not only assumed the non-linear passage of power and data but at the same time provided a structure into which the vertical legs of the system could be connected.

The inspiration for such a floor came from printed electronic circuit boards and the way a unique array of elements can connect with architectural rigour yet still appear random and elemental. The resultant structural metamorphosis of the system – from a steel tile matrix floor to a lightweight alloy leg that supported a polymer honeycomb surface plane – described a new environment that celebrated dematerialism, structural beauty and the economy of technological investment.

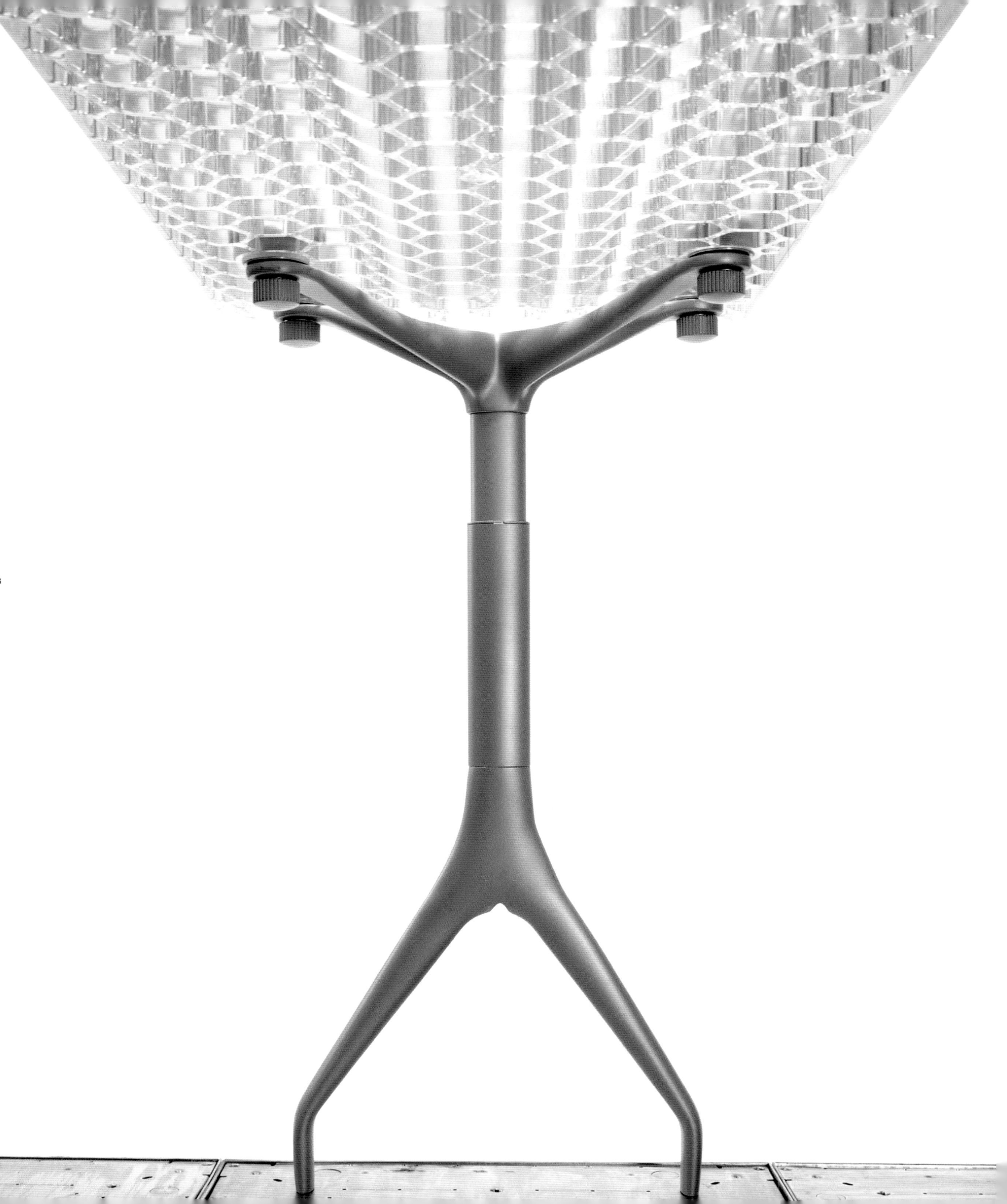

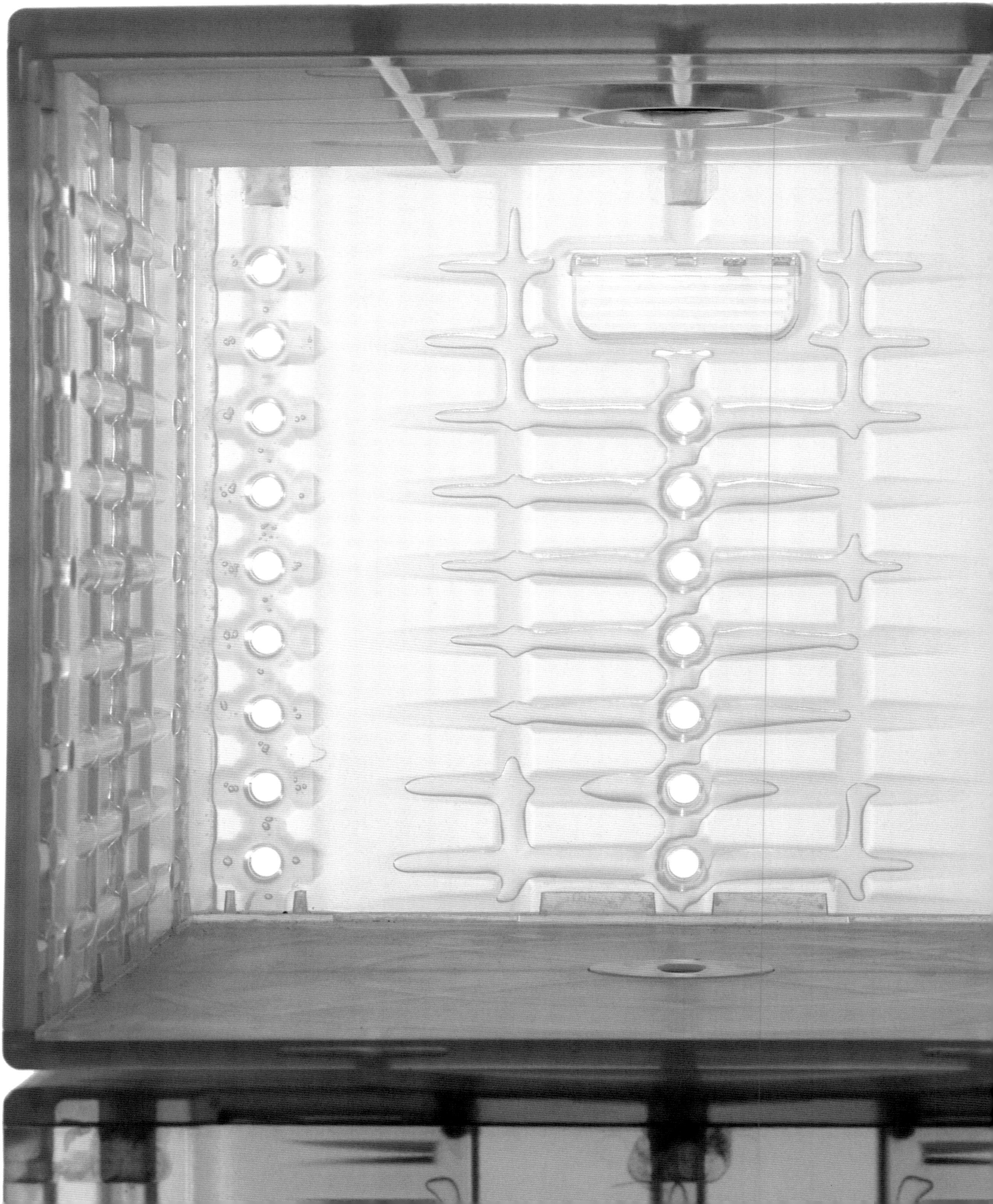

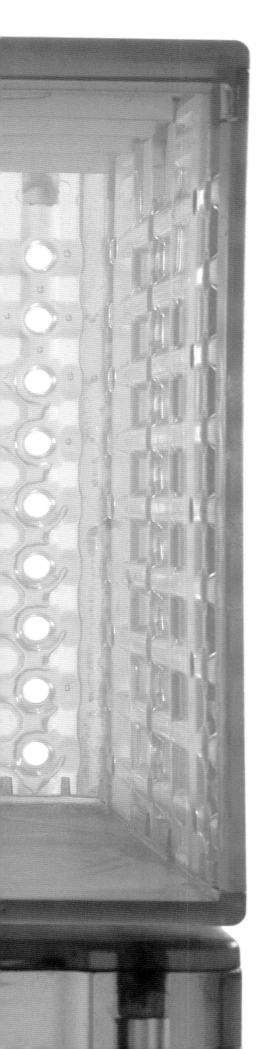

This was only made possible by the use of advanced polymers in the manufacture of work-surfaces and storage cubes. Such polymers can provide, with great logic and efficiency, lean and functional structures that are very close to nature in their conciseness. The polymers used to create such components were from the family of high-impact polystyrenes that, when injection-moulded in the form of developed honeycombs, can be up to four times more resistant to structural failure than their wood composite equivalents.

The development of the cube storage elements demanded an even greater level of lightness due to their portability, and so the HIPS (High-Impact Polystyrene) material was filled in its structural ribbing with an inert gas to reduce density and promote lightness. Once operational, the entire office scape could be changed in its colour by light. This was made possible by the interplay between the crystalline nature of the honeycomb and light sources that could be programmed to adapt throughout the working day to provide a biologically synergetic ambience unlike anything experienced in the office before.

This interplay between the physical and non-physical can lead to the creation of polysensorial environments that can have positive psychological effects upon people's health and wellbeing. The work undertaken on this programme has opened up new avenues of study and speculation for me. Indeed the industrial world, in order to be more efficient and purposeful, needs to embrace systems thinking in all fields, especially architecture and car design. Systems thinking means the intelligent assembly of modular components, ever standardized, that can facilitate a wide variety of form and structure, depending on their scale and geometry of assembly.

In 1999 I was approached by a ceramics company in Porto to design a private villa that would also function as a showcase for advanced ceramic building components, a field of inventing and manufacturing they wished to enter. They had previously seen a pavilion I had constructed from a foam ceramic process developed by me in collaboration with the Ceramic Network in Limoges, France.

They shared a belief in the re-emergence of ceramics in the building industry, inspired by new formulas and sophisticated high-precision manufacturing processes including injection-moulding and sintering with polymers. The intended site was directly on the coast with an uninterrupted view out to sea in a remote area.

My approach was to identify a single process that was suitable for a number of materials so that I could achieve a material transition related to light and the structure's ultimate function. I chose extrusion technology as a principle that was in itself a simple yet highly successful method of obtaining structure and volume relatively cheaply. Used vertically one could achieve walls that were not only straight and provided excellent structural integrity through compression, but that could be assembled from a variety of extruded materials from aluminium through to ceramic, polycarbonate and glass.

Viewed from the side the structure begins with aluminium as the housing for the car and then morphs via material transition into alumina ceramic, opaline polycarbonate, transparent polycarbonate and then finally glass where it draws in the light from the sea.

The floor inside the building follows the same approach, but the holes that are

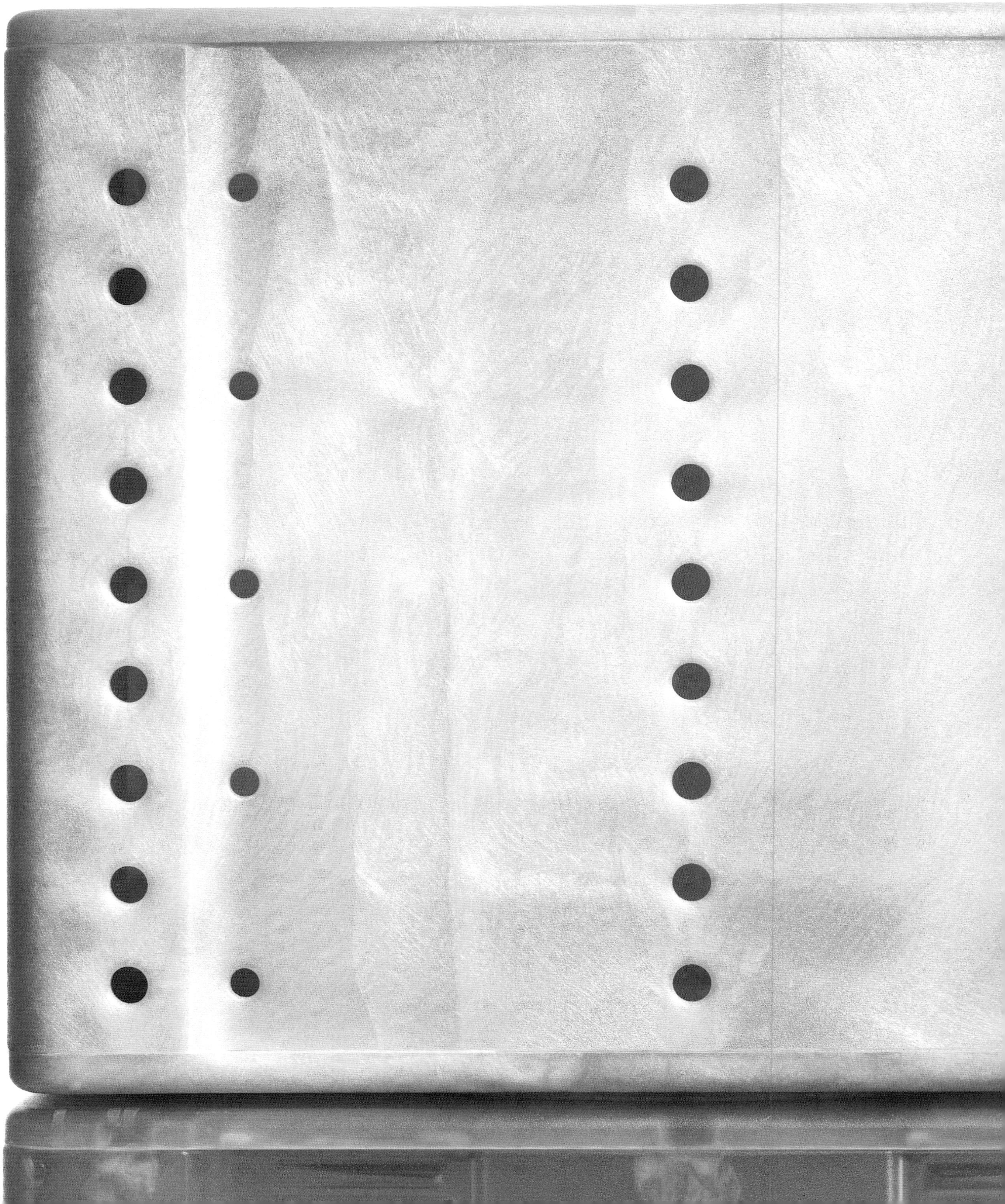

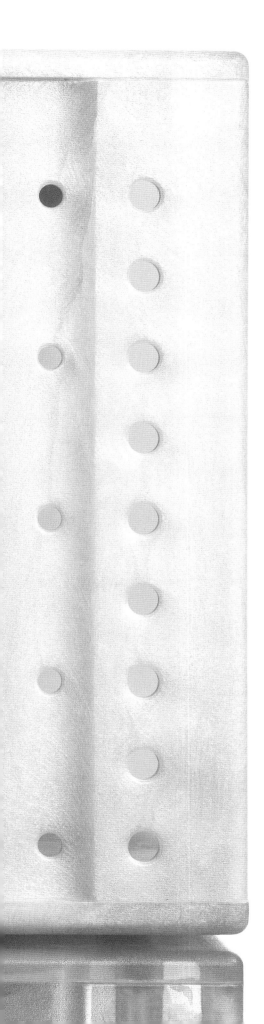

created by a short tube matrix are filled with a variety of materials from silicone to wool as the functions of the internal zones change from wet to dry. This undulating and rich geometry and its material transition defines a new approach in the creation of single-process, multiple-material structures from which an almost infinite variety of floor mapping can be created.

'Systems can be envisaged which consist of some minimum inventory of component types which can be alternatively combined to yield a great diversity of efficient structural forms ... By such a "system" I mean a minimalized inventory of component types (a kit of parts) ... minimum inventory/maximum diversity.'[8]
Peter Pearce

Most of my concepts for architecture to date such as Solar Seed, Villa Matoso or Tube Architecture have sought out a component logic in the processes employed for piece-part manufacture in order to achieve either the reduction of material density, the expression of variable geometry or to propose ways that industrial design thinking can influence the economics of constructing large polymer structures. I continue actively to study the possibility of technology transfer, from product to automotive to architectural. For example, relating the knowledge gained developing products such as the transit furniture for bdlove.com made from roto-moulded polyethylene, to the creation of a one-piece integrated body of a car or the modulated stacking of repeated units to form colourful building systems.

Almost all of the processes and materials I encounter – the polymer components developed for Herman Miller, the PET Waterbottle for Ty Nant, the foam furniture for Edra and the roto-moulded street furniture developed for bdlove.com – I study further in order to find ways to adapt them later to create projects that challenge the way we conceive and perceive our future built environment.

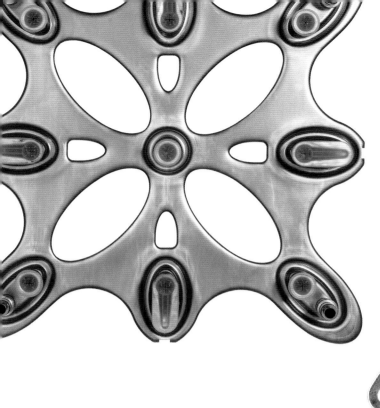

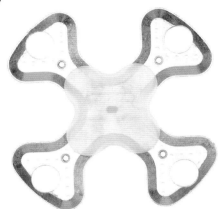

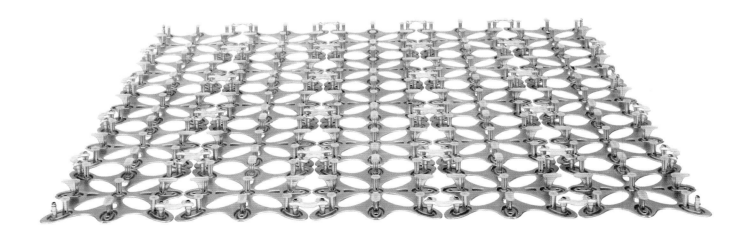

  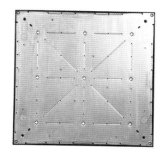

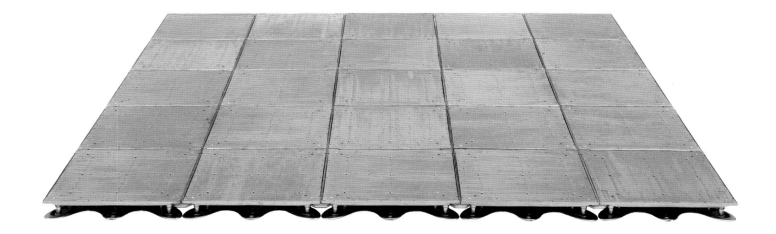

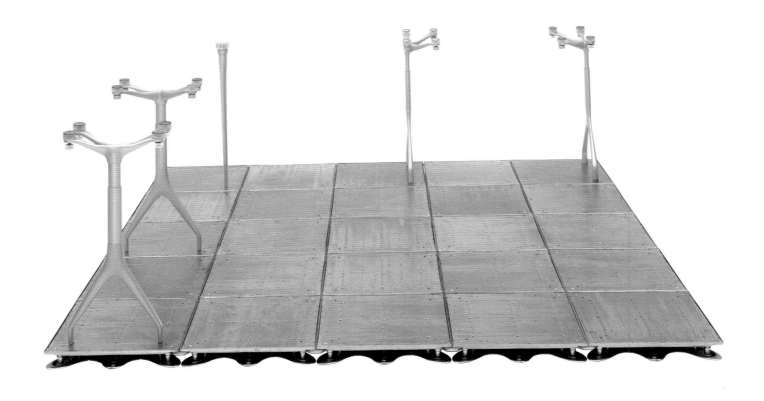

'One characteristic of successful systems will be that the rubrics –
the rules of assemblage – and the physical components themselves
will be seen to be organically related: the rules will be seen to grow
out of the parts, the parts out of the rules.'[9] Peter Pearce

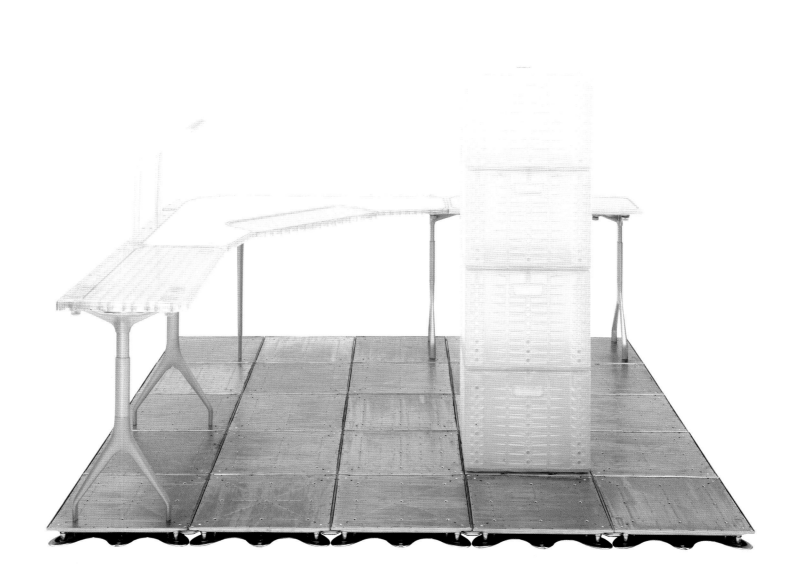

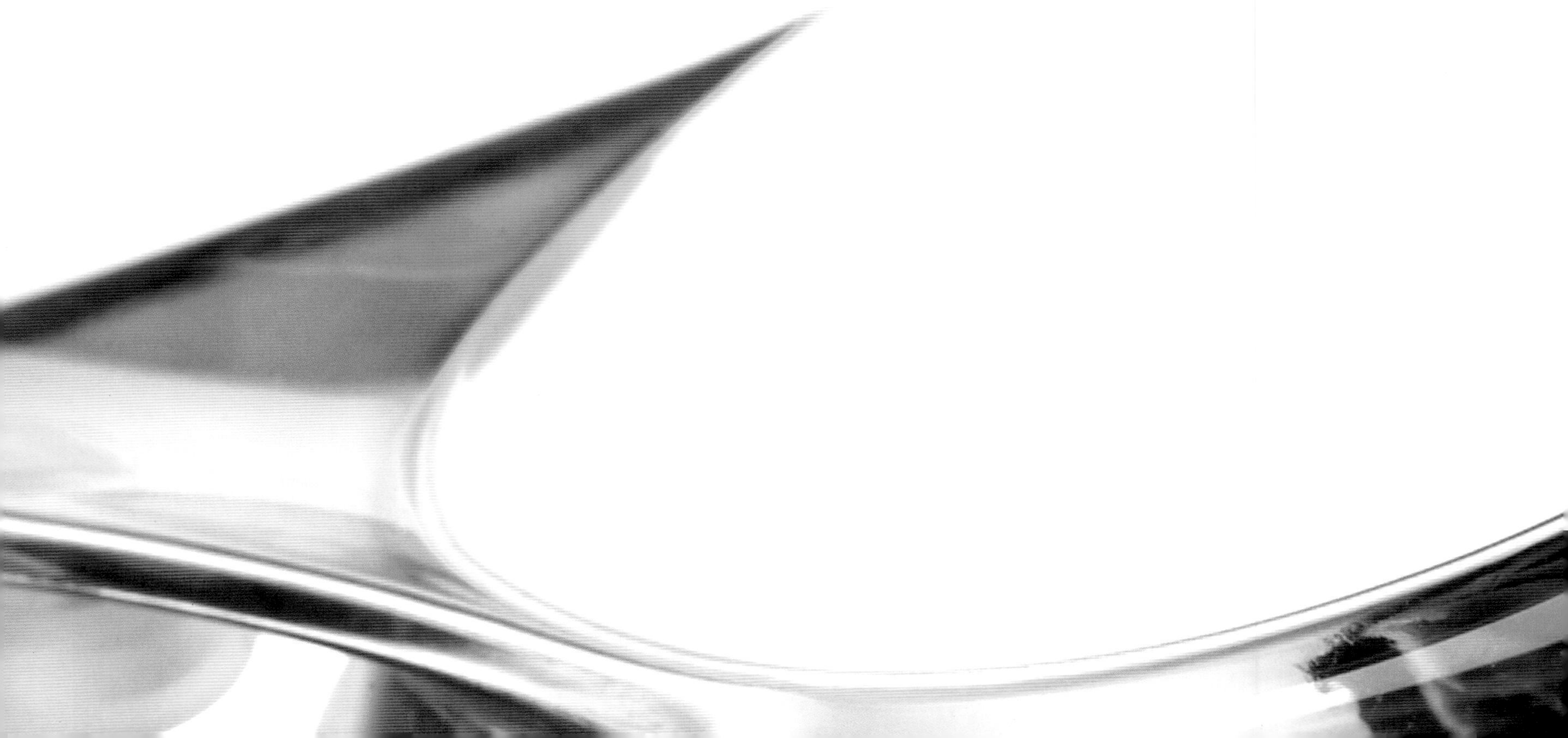

Swimming Goggles – by Nike

Injection-moulded polycarbonate,
silicone rubber and surface-coating
technology.

Developed by Nike, this is, for
Lovegrove, an inspirational product
and represents his interest in
emerging mixed material products and
their technocracy.

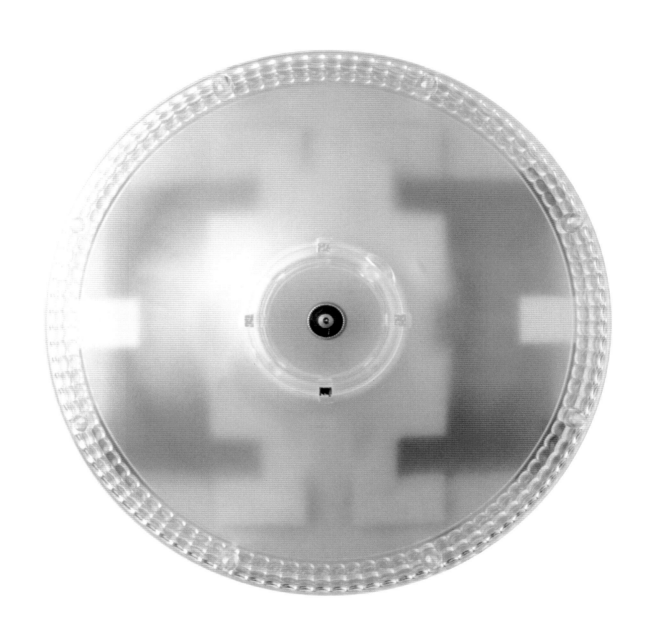

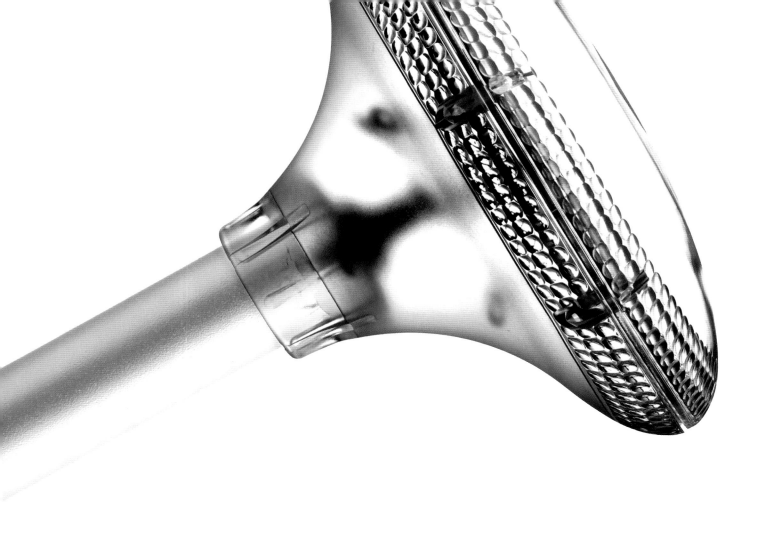

'*Inspired by better materials for lightweight structures and by new materials supported by scientific research, Lovegrove's creative and conscious approach reflects an awareness of environmental and sustainable issues.*'[16] Alberto Meda

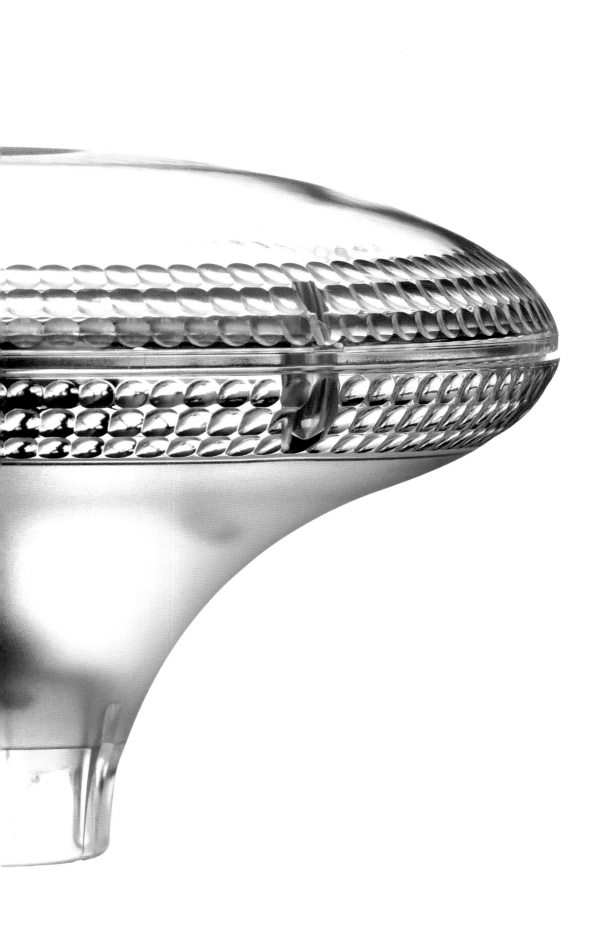

Agaricon Table Light

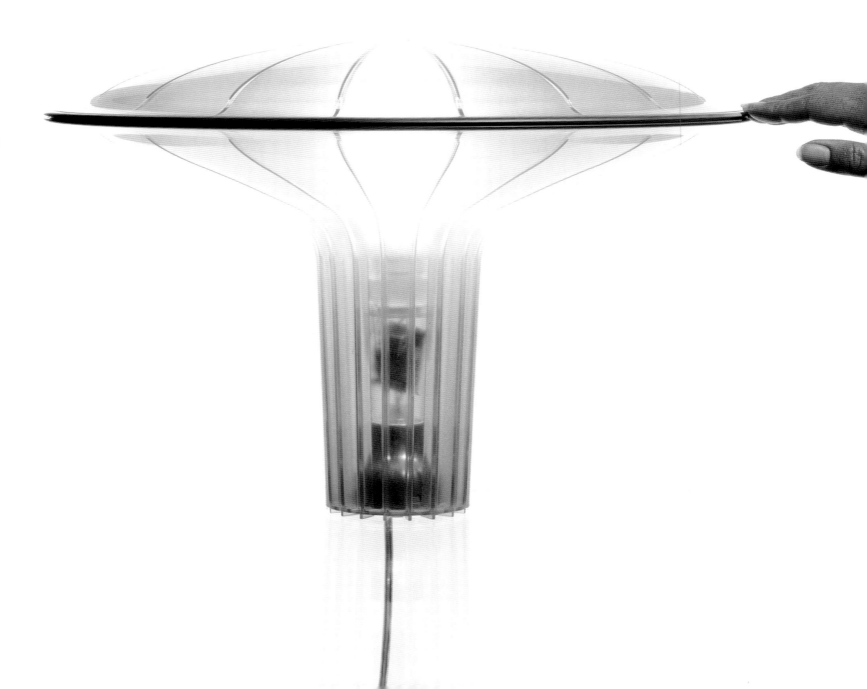

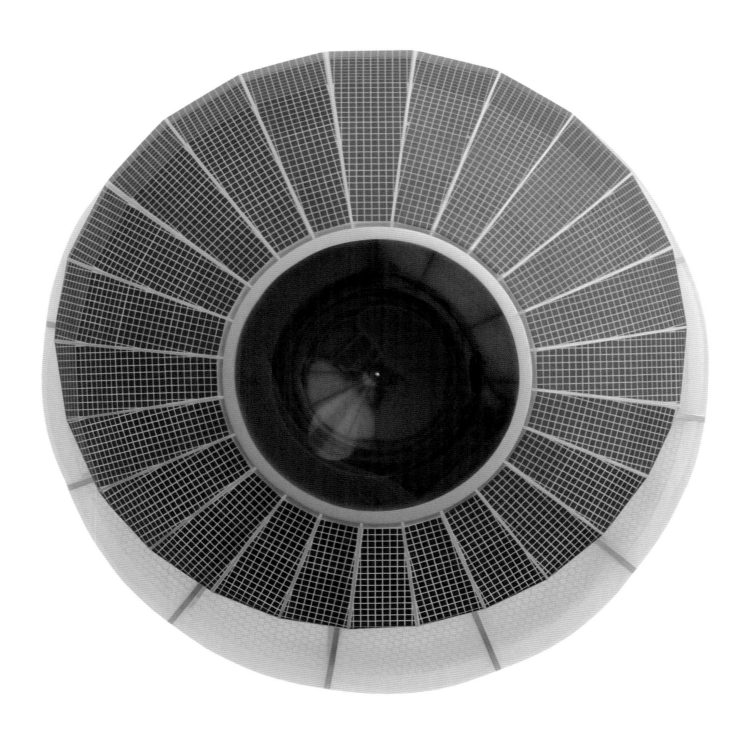

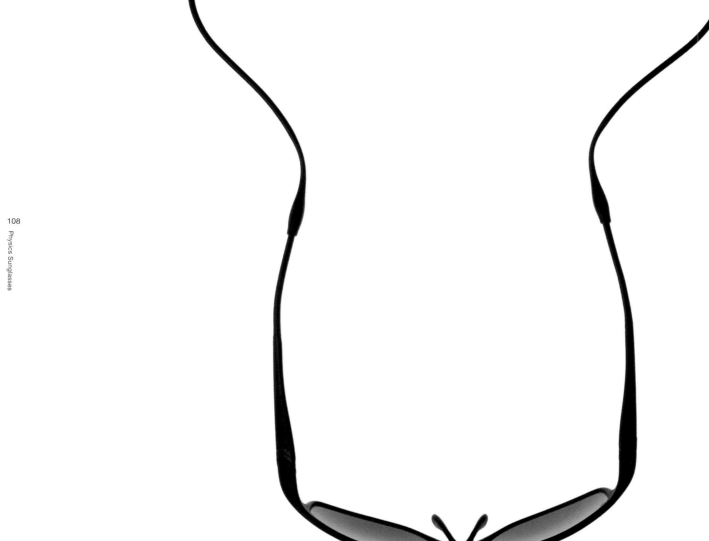

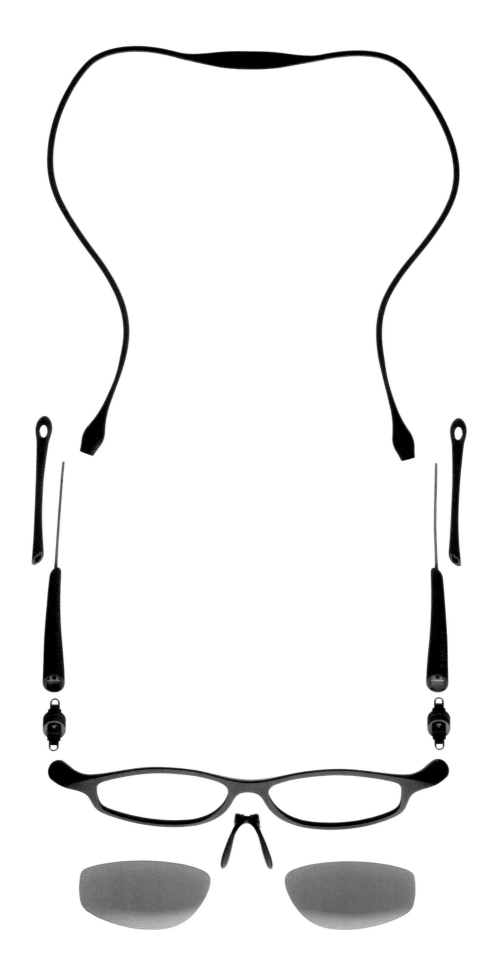

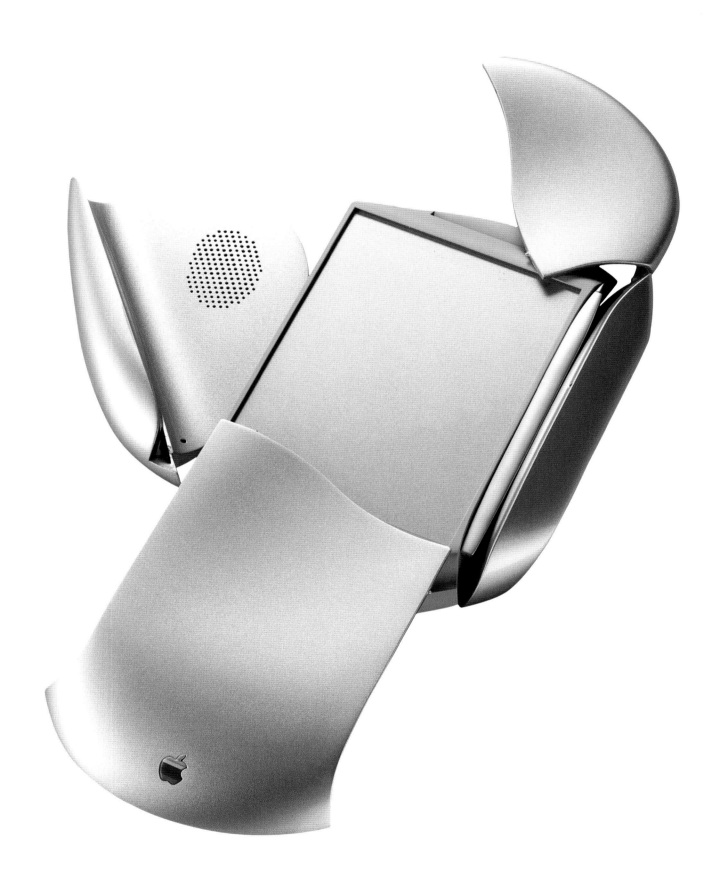

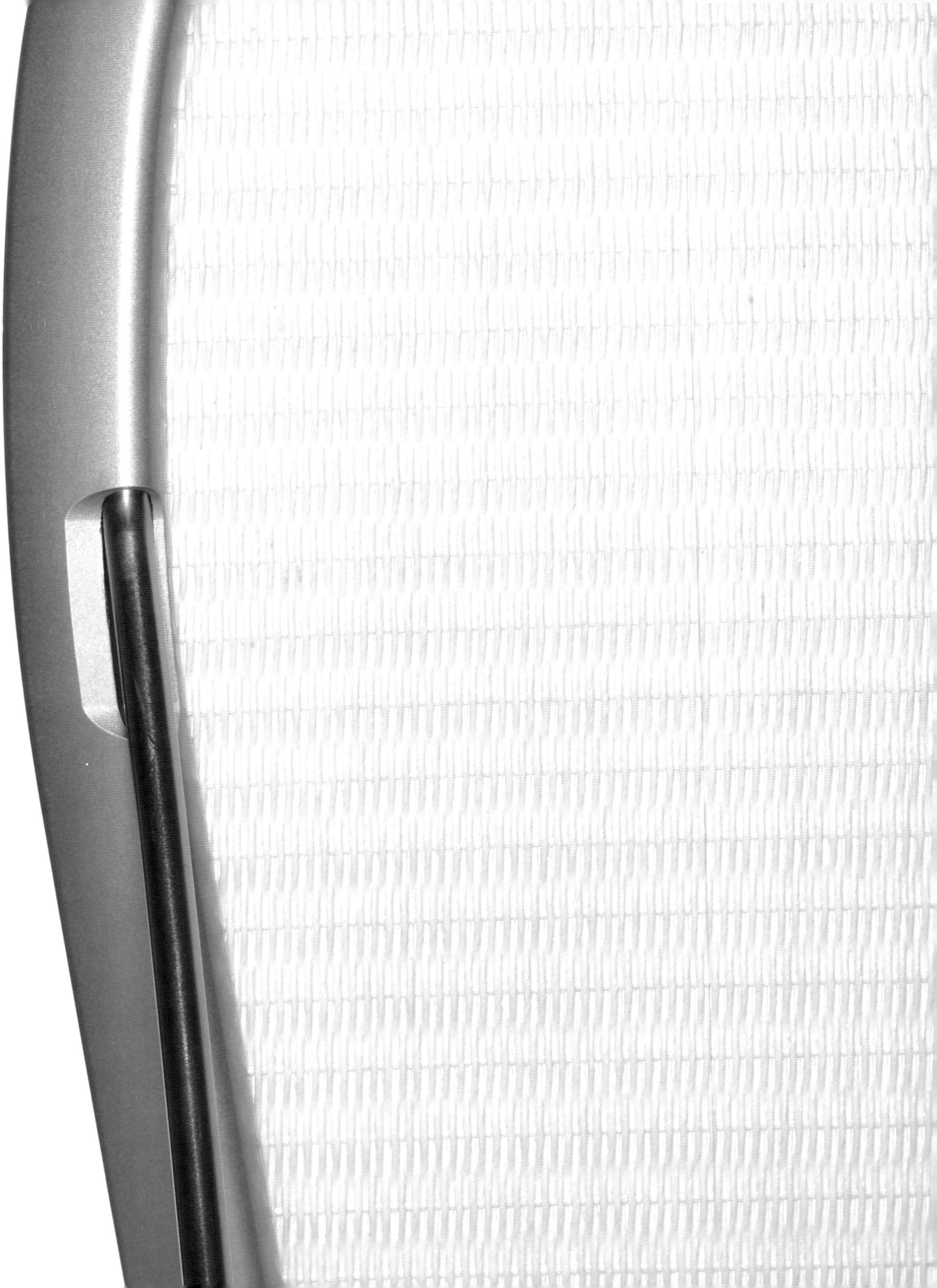

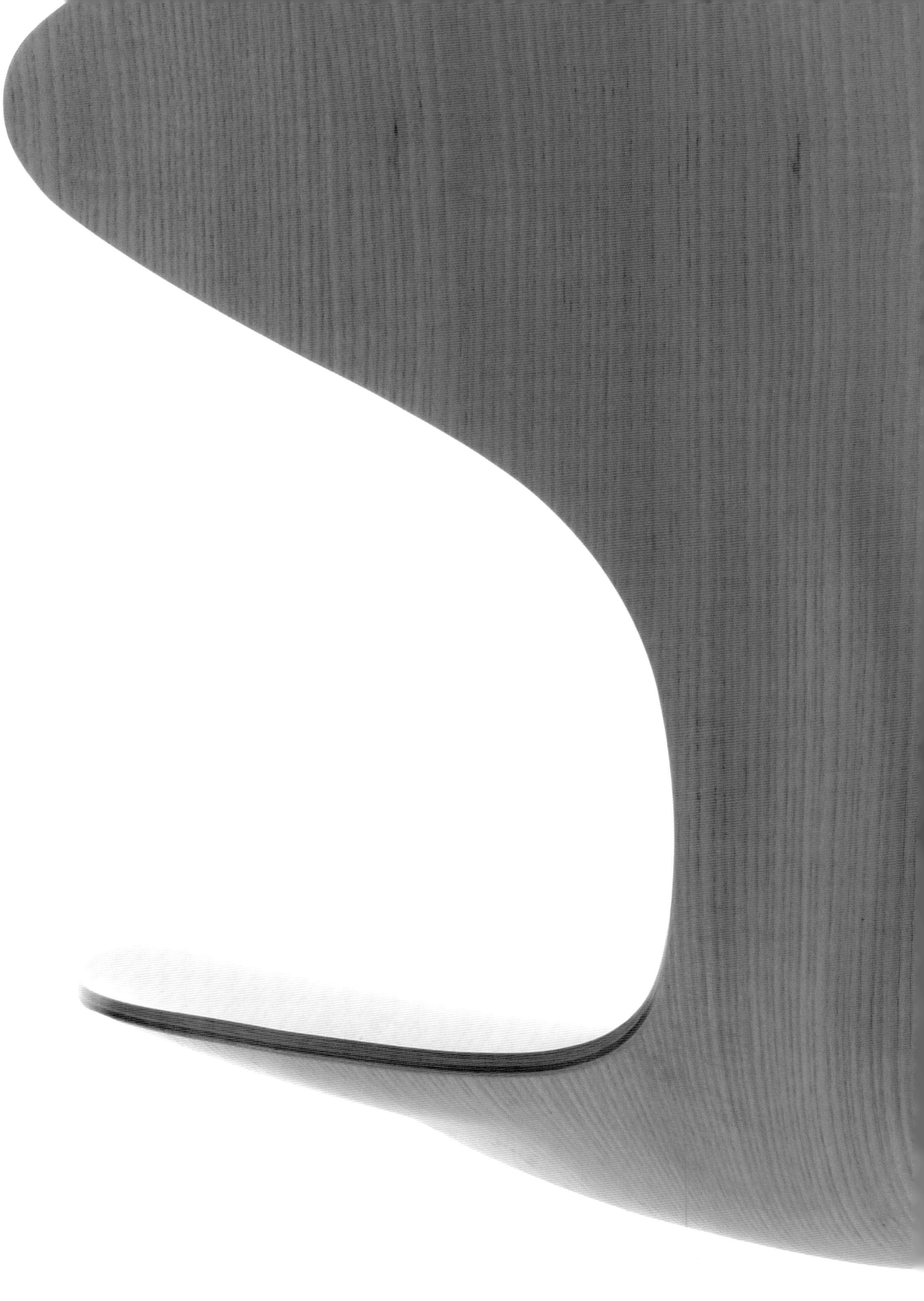

Orbit Plywood Chair (Flyply)

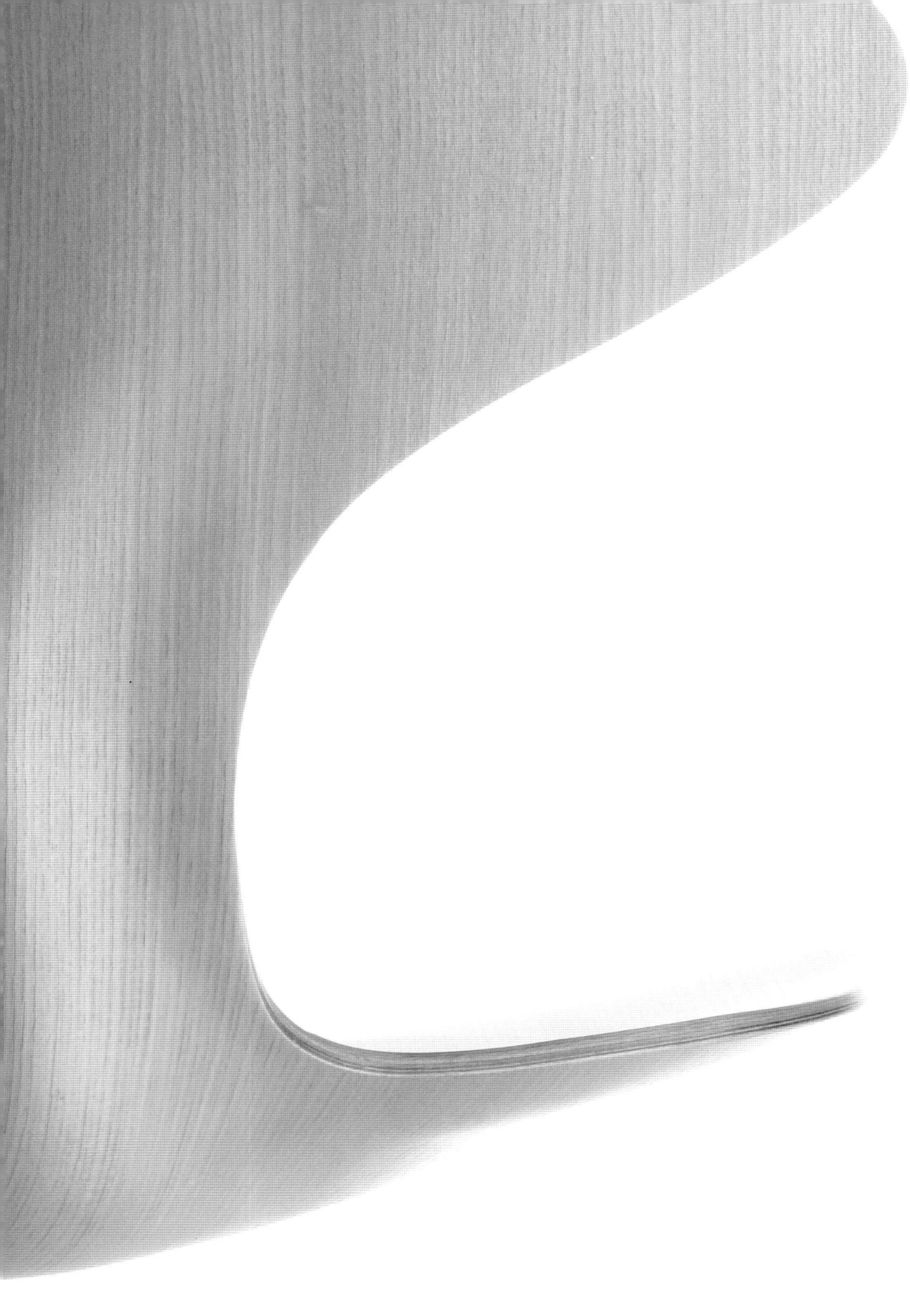

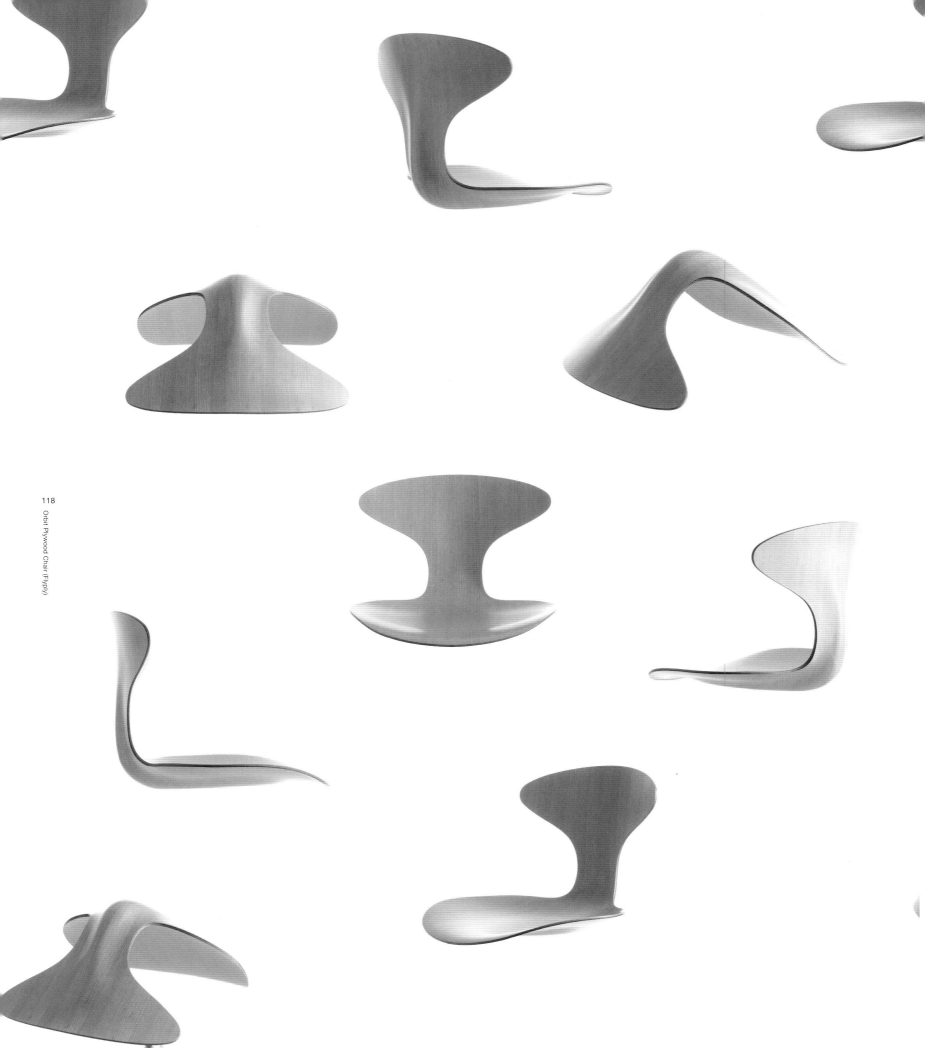

Orbit Plywood Chair (Flyply)

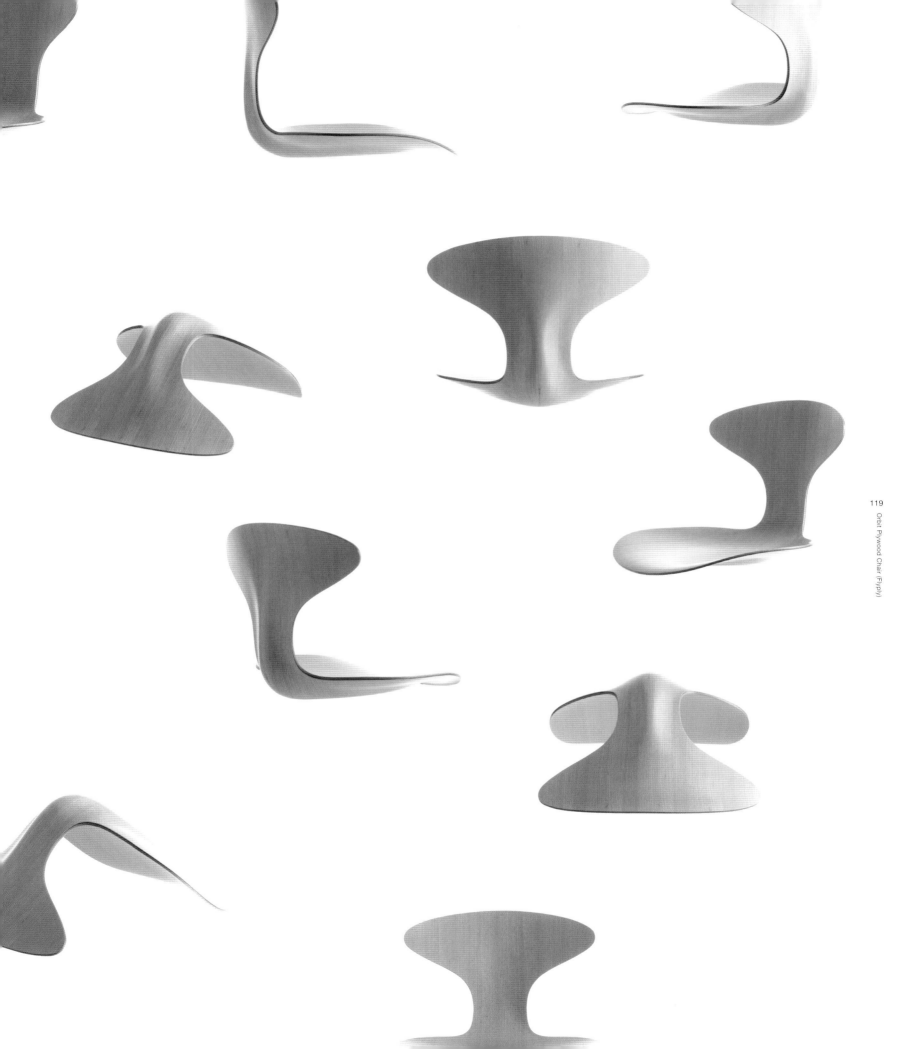

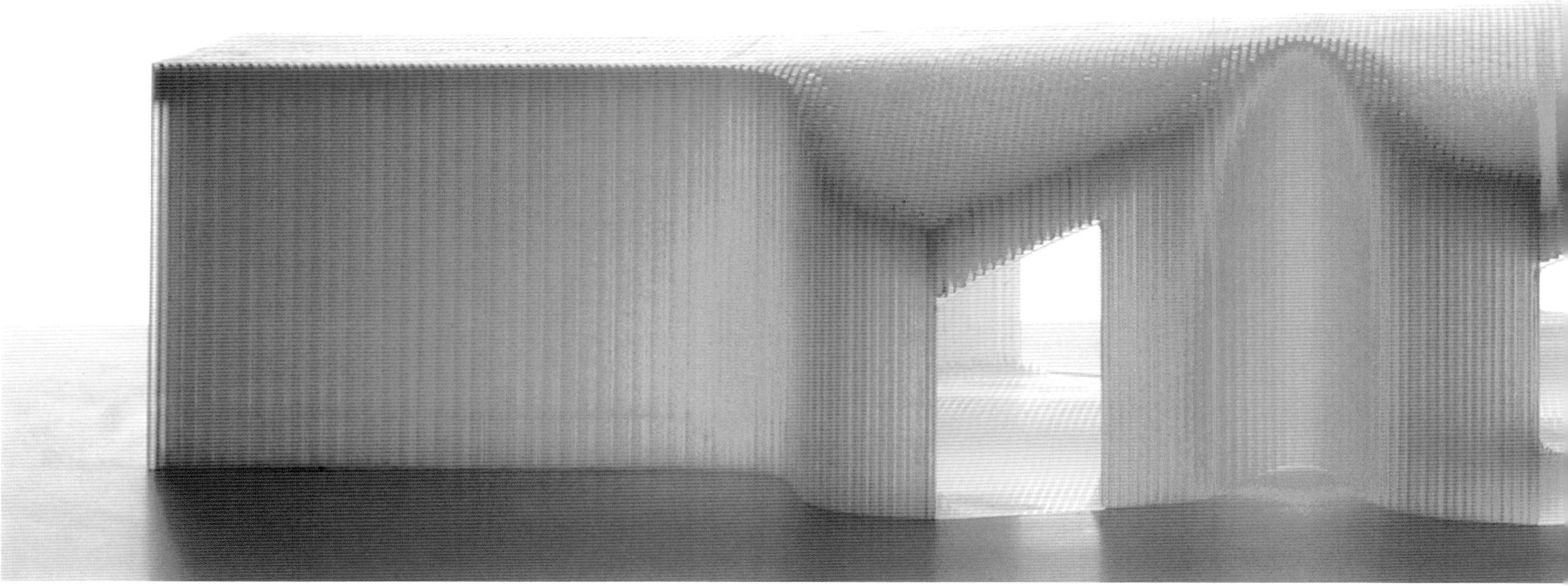

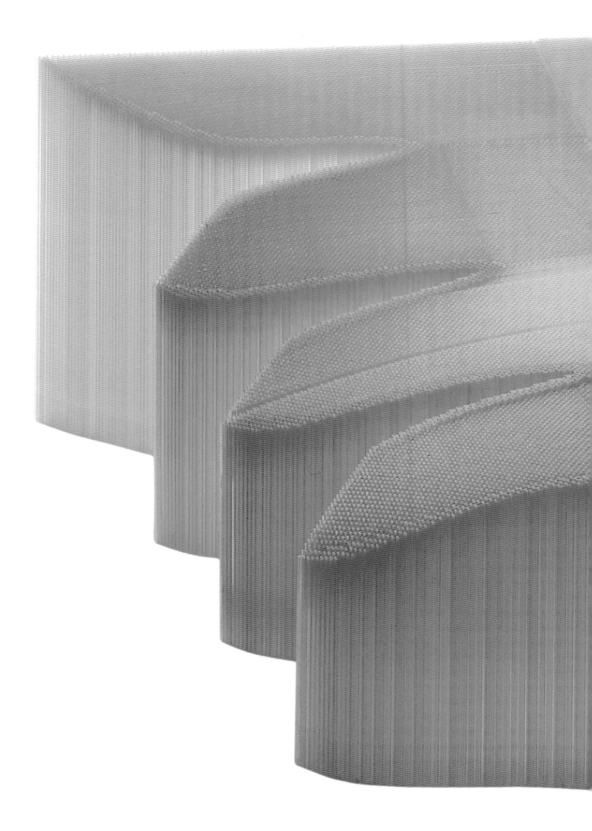

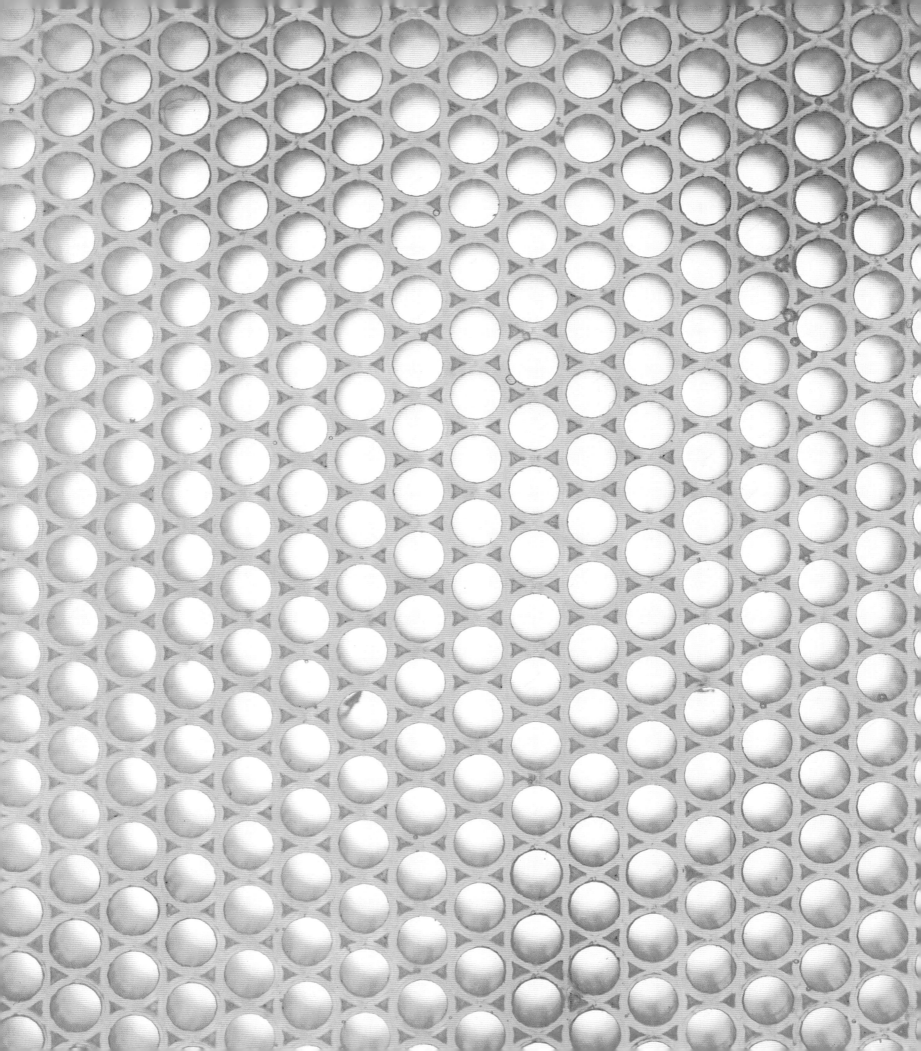

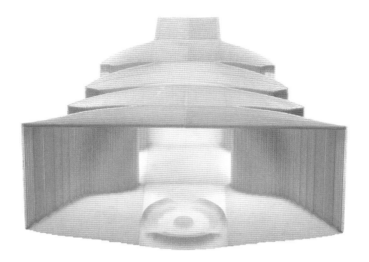

Taut, Seamless, Opalescent by Greg Lynn

Tautness is typically the quality of reading a tensile force in the shape, colour and consistency of a form. There is no such thing as a taut straight line. Tautness comes from inflexion. Ross's work is always curved and his best work is the tautest. This is a simple tautology supported, for example, by the Go Chair. Tautness also implies that there is some stored energy, like the camber in a skateboard that can be tapped for its latent force.

From the scale of the Go Chair to the Physics Sunglasses, Ross's objects are made out of multiple materials in moulds and this introduces the need to think about seams and connections. These and many other of his projects have monolithic aspirations. The co-injection, fusing, bonding and inlaying of multiple materials produces monolithic forms with razor-thin seams. The gradient transition of hard magnesium/aluminum to flexible plastic in the frame of the Tag Heuer sunglasses is a virtuoso example of this.

Flexible structural stiffness is not a quality of hard structures but of more elastic hard materials. The DNA staircase not only integrates the disparate functions of tread, riser, post and hand-rail into one surface but is attenuated and tapered for flexion and stiffness like a cartilaginous structure.

Ross's default neutral palette is glowing translucent ambers and bleached natural materials. Take the plastic organic ambers of the tubes that were proposed for the Villa Matoso as an example. He highlights these materials with various matte finished metals. When he works in gloss finishes his aesthetic is always opalescence but usually his whites are what he refers to as *silky*, meaning they have reflective silvers behind a matte finish, giving luminous depth without causing reflection.

Bamboo Storage
Linder Garland's Bamboo Foundation
Ubud, Bali

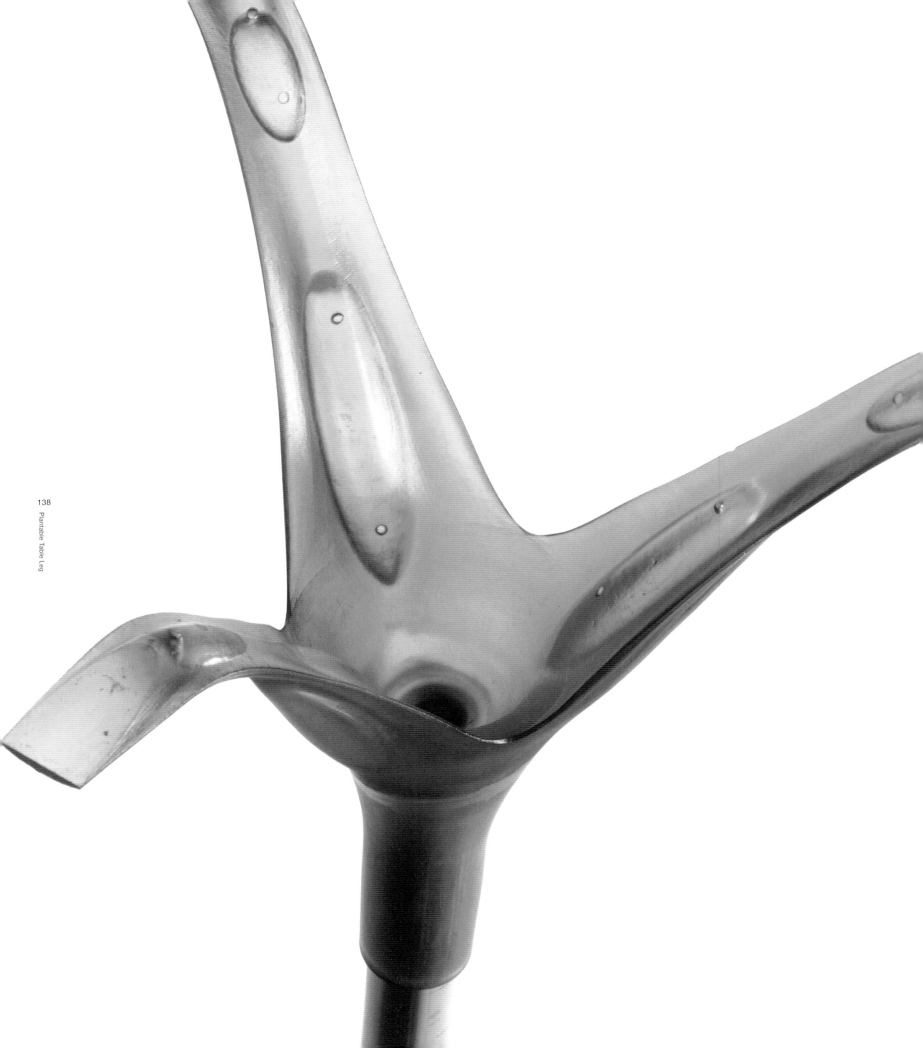

Elemental by Cecil Balmond

Without material where would we be? Lost and incoherent, in a world of nothing. There would be no glass, metal or wood; no plastics, no textiles and no molecules. From the unseen nano-world of structured patterns to the macro-built forms of brick, stone, steel, the substance around us informs and educates. Metaphors arise. Our arguments are solid like concrete, friends stick like glue, threats melt away, the truth stretches like rubber. A person's character is transparent. As we take the stress and strain of work, our lives become hard-pressed. Smoothness, softness, striation, tangled and knotted, webbed, notions of materiality shape and flesh out our sensory language. We are guided, informed, teased and tortured by material. We hate it. We love it. For we are *it*!

The mass and contour of our bodies achieves a brilliant bilateral symmetry defining the rational vertical and horizontal during waking hours. But then the unknown enters in dreams and folds and tucks into our mind mysterious and fantastic strands, forging other materials, new imaginations. One is embedded in the other. Behind the surface and textures – dense, porous, fluorescent, fibrous – the deeper memory catches at instinct and poetry.

Body and muscle too has fabric – collagen and tissue that stretch or compress, yielding or resisting, those mechanical efficiencies translating into litheness, grace, as the human figure drapes or folds in action. The literal, through the material medium, is again transcended. The cosmos is part of this play. All matter when just born has a bias, quarks have left- or right-hand spins – from there by unknown bifurcations of chance and seemingly a material will to cohere, the stars and planets and universe form. That most secret engine, gravity, is itself a weave, a tapestry of intimate force lines held by the stellar masses. And today we still detect that original spin as the galaxies continue to spiral. All around is material, transforming itself, into the spirit of things.

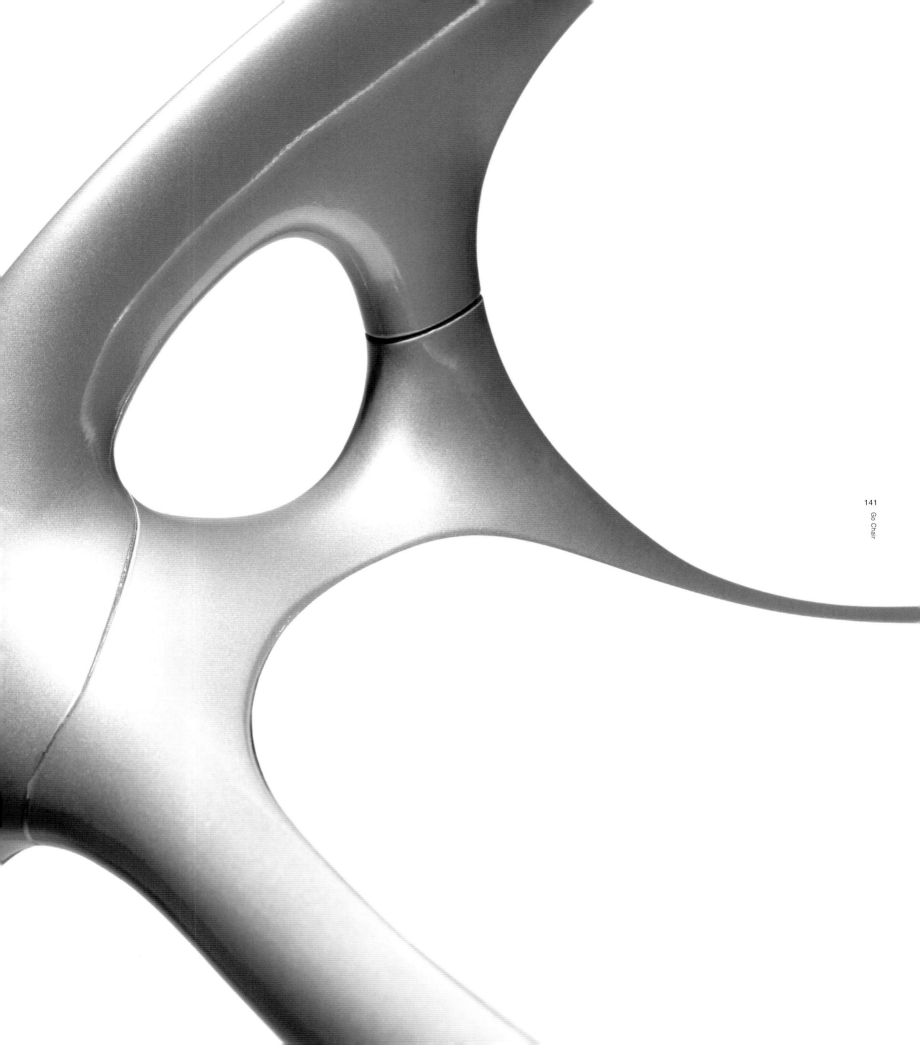

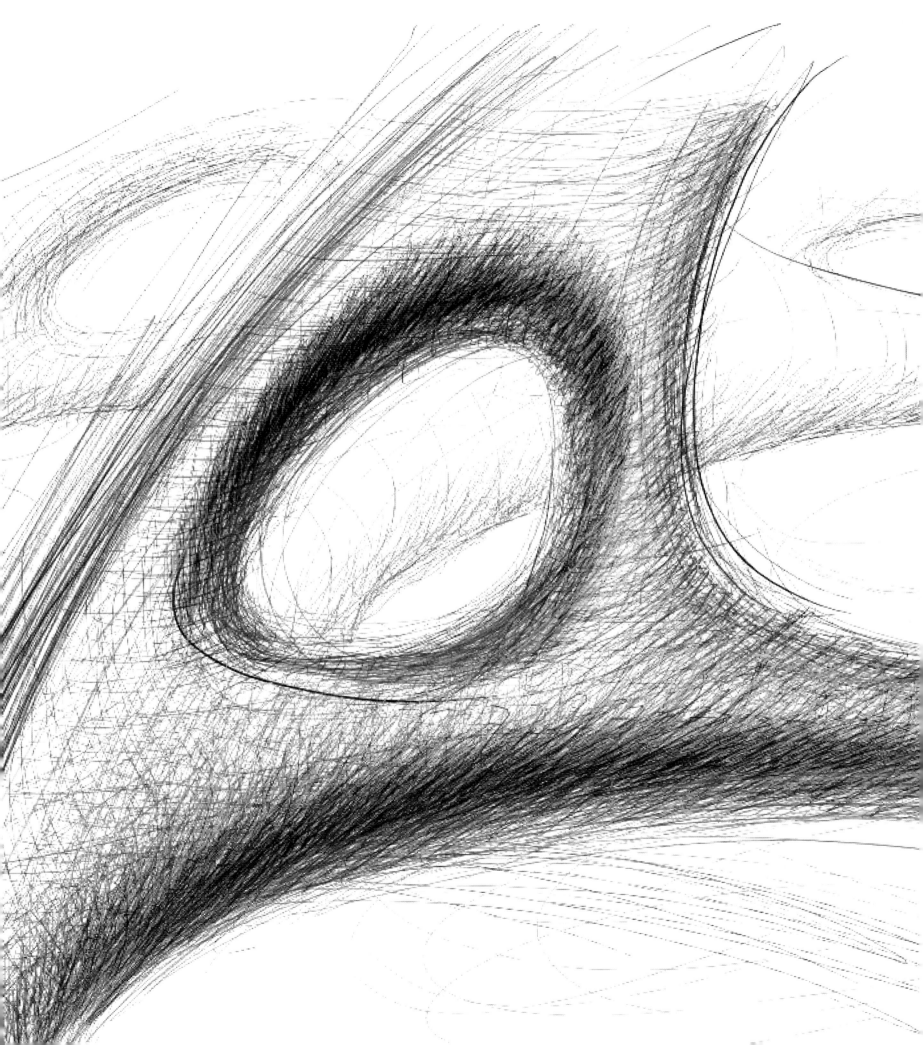

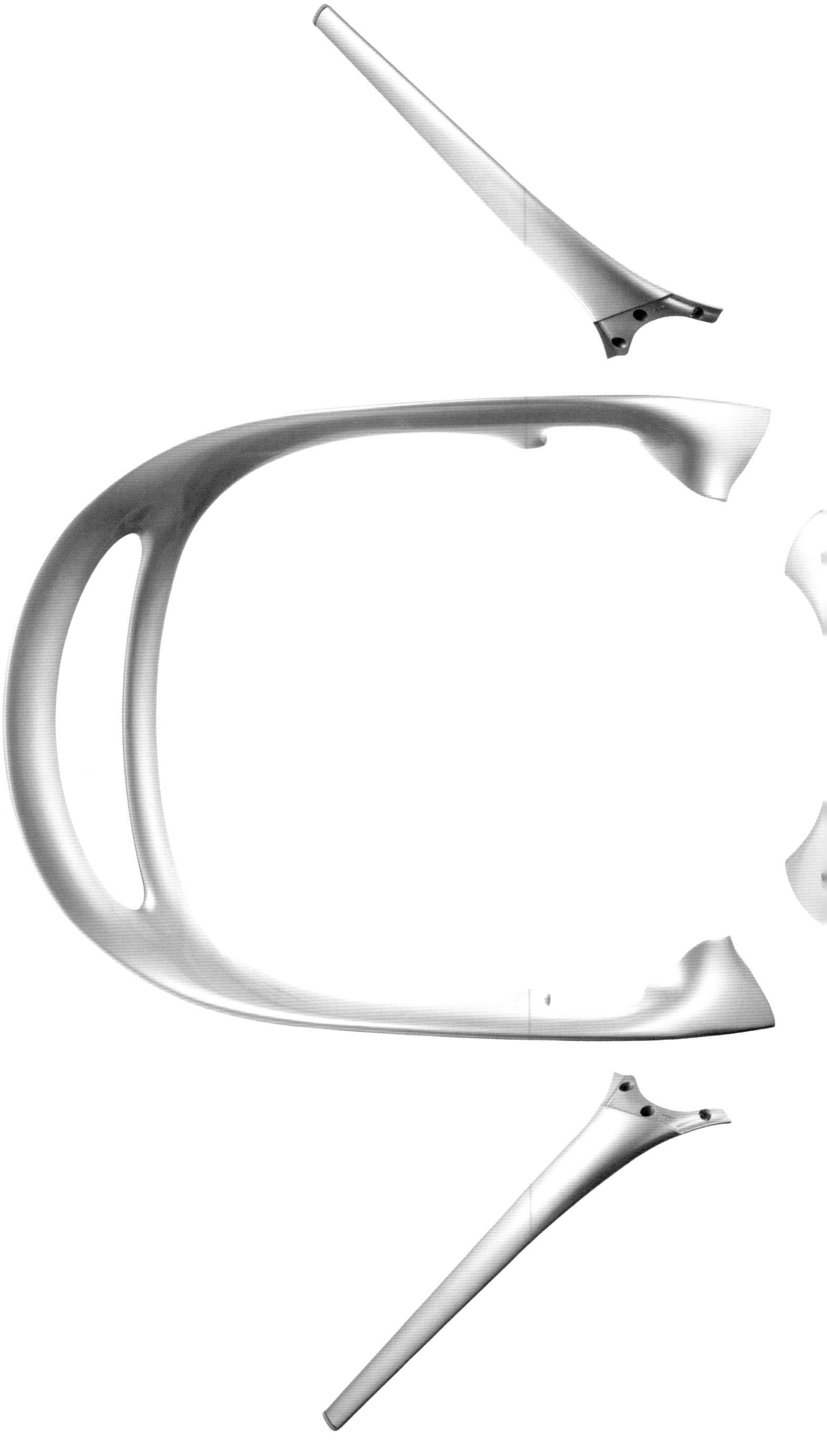

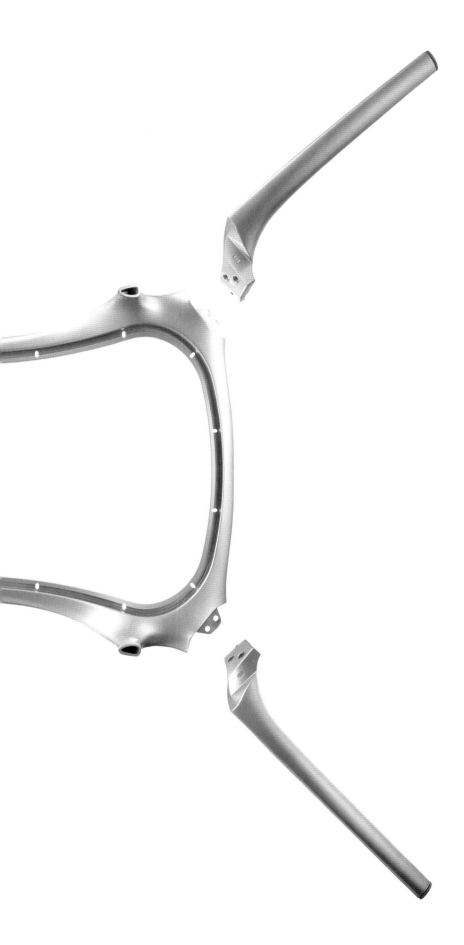

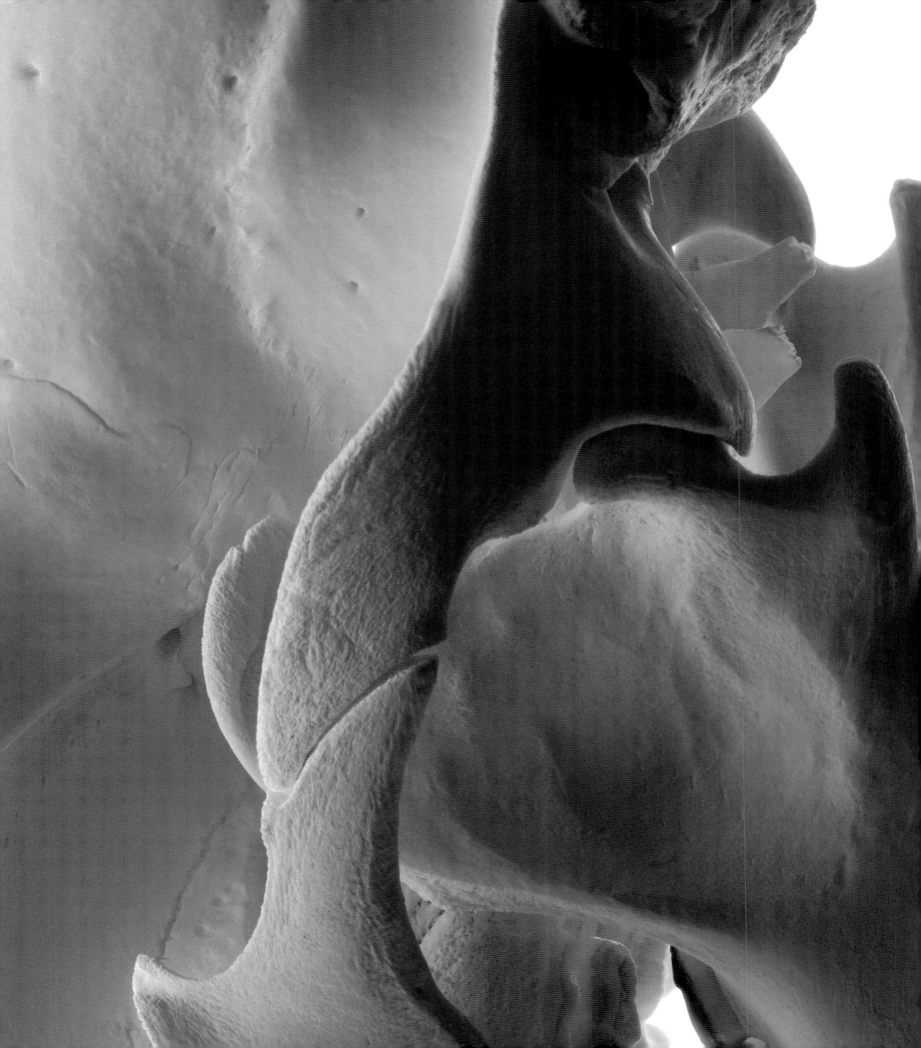

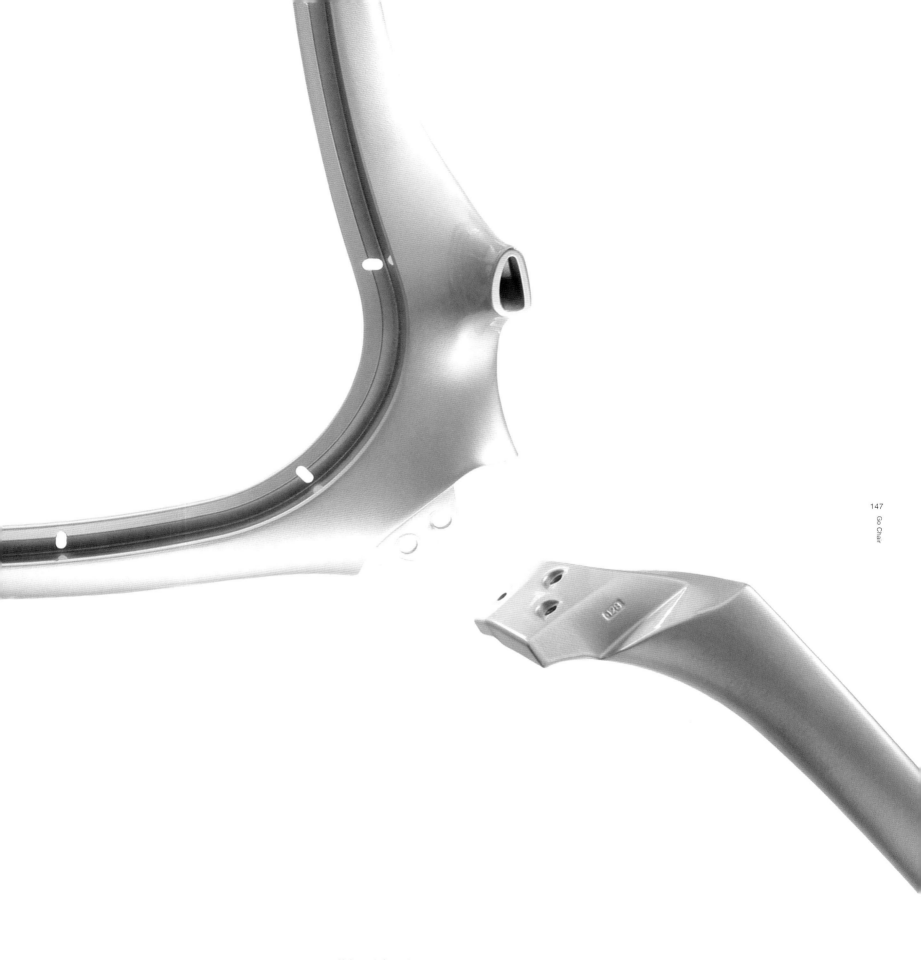

'Hard body parts made from a mixture of inorganic minerals and organic polymers ... your bones are crystals of calcium phosphate deposited in a polymer matrix.'[12] Janine M Benyus

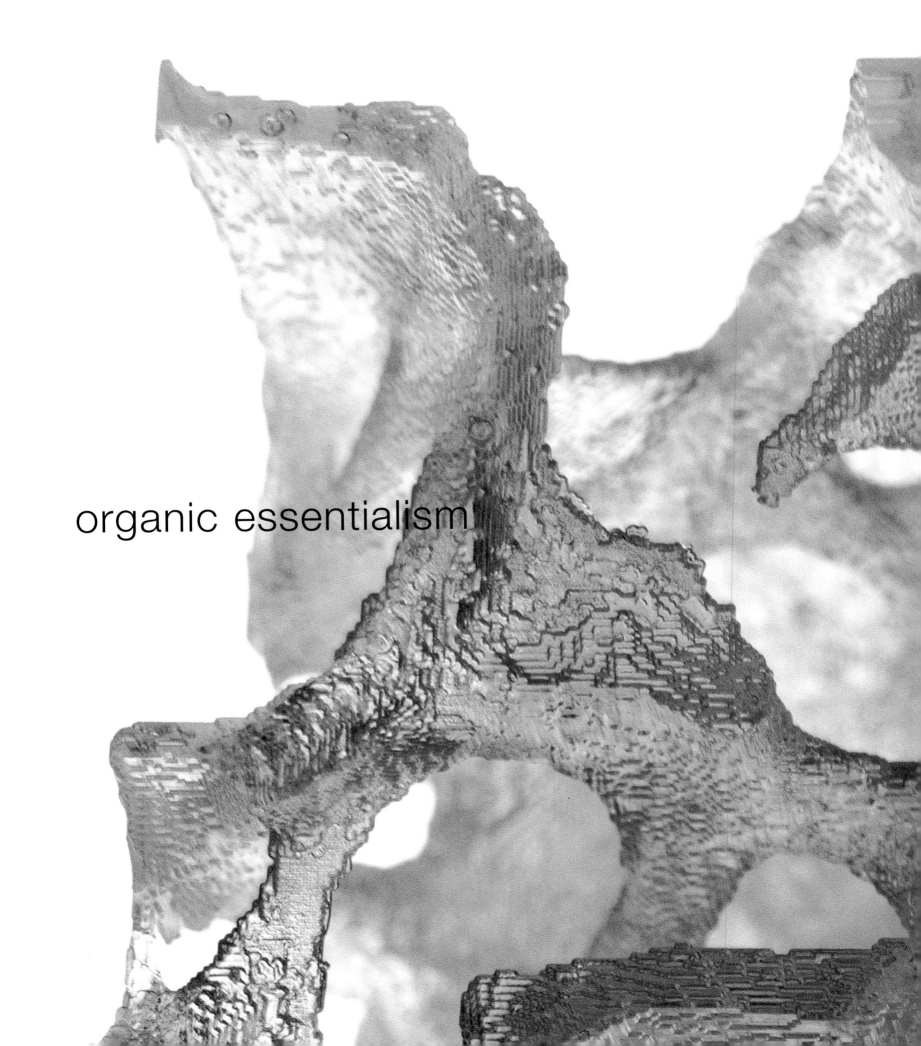

organic essentialism

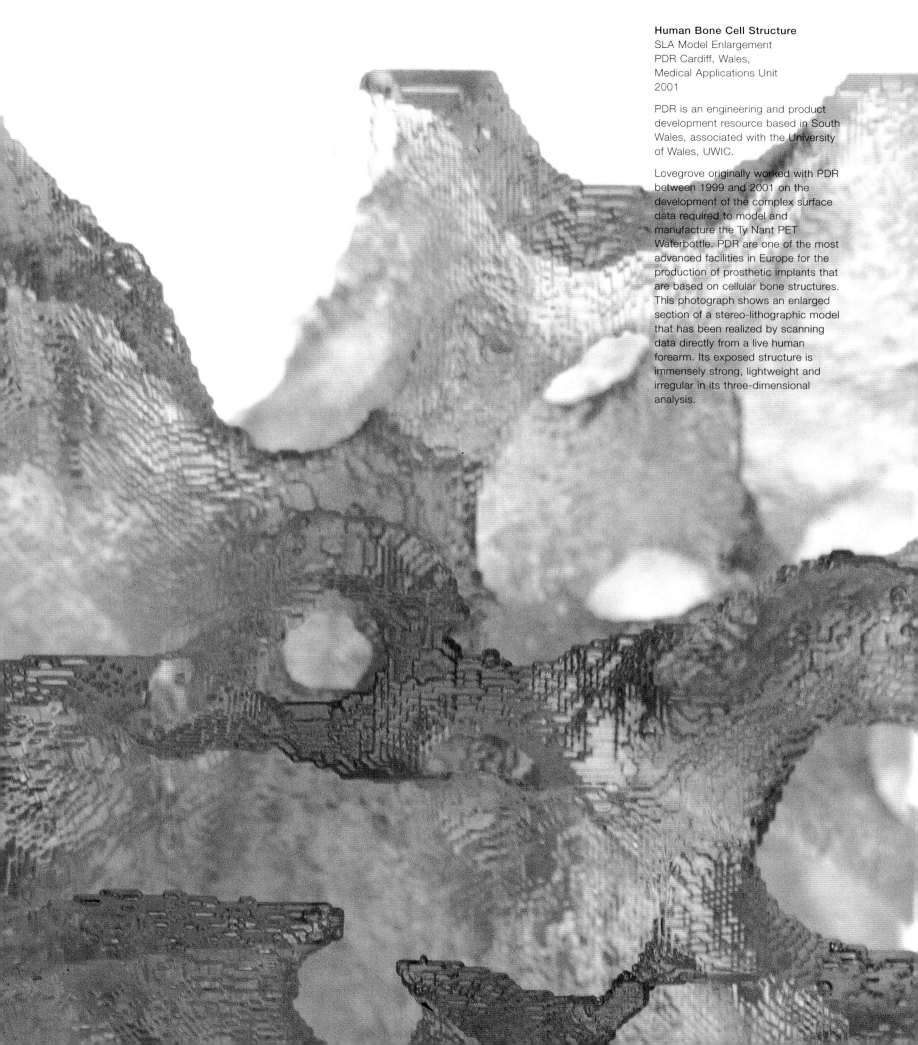

Human Bone Cell Structure
SLA Model Enlargement
PDR Cardiff, Wales,
Medical Applications Unit
2001

PDR is an engineering and product development resource based in South Wales, associated with the University of Wales, UWIC.

Lovegrove originally worked with PDR between 1999 and 2001 on the development of the complex surface data required to model and manufacture the Ty Nant PET Waterbottle. PDR are one of the most advanced facilities in Europe for the production of prosthetic implants that are based on cellular bone structures. This photograph shows an enlarged section of a stereo-lithographic model that has been realized by scanning data directly from a live human forearm. Its exposed structure is immensely strong, lightweight and irregular in its three-dimensional analysis.

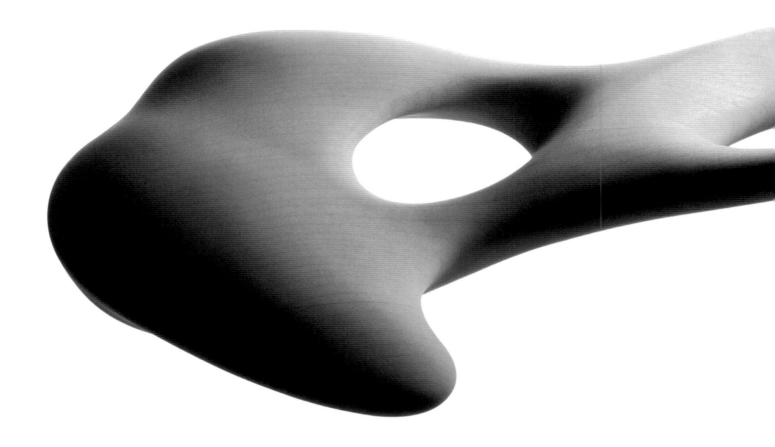

'All forms in nature are determined by the interaction of intrinsic with extrinsic forces.' [13] Peter Pearce

There is no simple methodology to achieve the balance of materials, technology and form, only a process of internalization of the object derived from an intuitive sensibility, designing from the inside out and outside in to find a harmony between all things considered.

Such objects are not instantaneously inspired but arrive at a time when the welling up of information is such that the act of design comes naturally, with the relevant forces acting upon the concept. To impose one's artificial aesthetic on the form makes it self-conscious and stylistic. To work from such preconceptions denies the possibility of creating something not seen or felt before in the purest sense.

I consider it a virtue to find a meaning in the existence of things, often imbuing the pieces I design with silent properties that touch people without words in an emotional way, originating from deep within the subconscious. The man-made artefacts that we used to create long ago in pre-history achieved such a rare status because they were born out of instinct and intuition as much as necessity.

These primordial, pre-linguistic tools still retain their deep inherent qualities because they were made initially as a spiritual act of reverence for hard-to-come-by materials, and their purposeful transformation into meaningful artefacts.

In our modern times the process of creation in the industrial world is becoming more and more detached from the origin of materials and processes. From this position a new generation of designers will need to emerge as translators of resources into industrial products. But they will need to have a new instinct that can relate the hyper-scientific technologies and their expressions to the deep sensorial origins of how we perceive the world around us.

The term 'organic essentialism' is only one way of expressing an approach to the

creation of forms in space. It is an economic combination of two factors, the 'organic' meaning structures that are fluid and uninterrupted and 'essentialism' being the search for the natural essence of a physical object in terms of its inherent combination of materials and form.

The term implies a connection between surface and content whereby the object is conceived by a layering that conveys stability, honesty and depth. This depth is something that resonates feeling and communicates the unaffected creation of something that feels balanced in the eyes of nature; something grown rather than constructed, programmed by a sense of evolution rather than contemporary aesthetics.

There are few industrial examples because it is rare to find solutions that have a sense of truth, evolved outside of the mainstream of commercial market manipulation, and that have a place in evolution because these are objects which demonstrate a 'naturalness' that transcends trends or affectation. However, these few exceptions display an inevitability that connects well with our sensorial perception of naturalness; achieved through the abstract forces of technology, its wonder and our need of it in combination with rooted evolutionary forms. This combination is the evocative essence of physicality that moves us.

'But even the purist geometry is not completely abstract, for the presence of geometric forms in nature evokes human responses and changes them with vital associations ... The organic can come out of the inorganic.'[14]
Isamu Noguchi, Japan

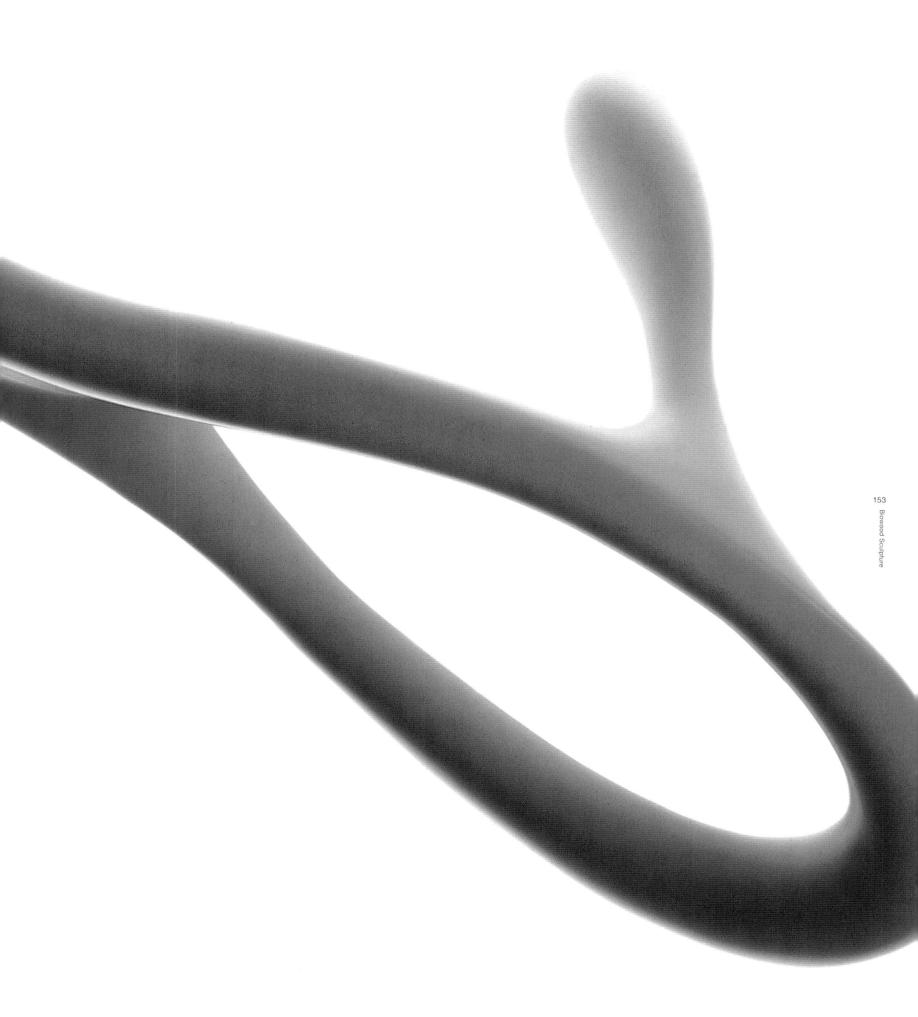

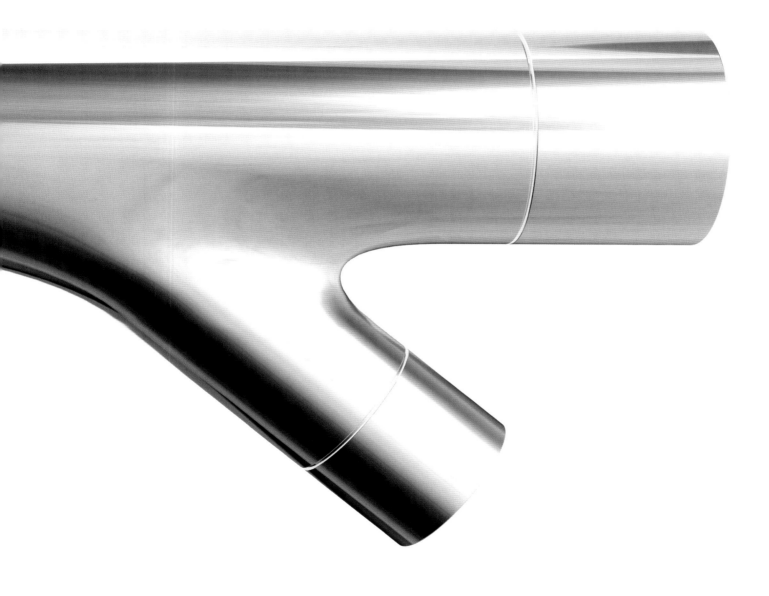

Solo Stainless Steel Cutlery

Ceramic Tea Pot

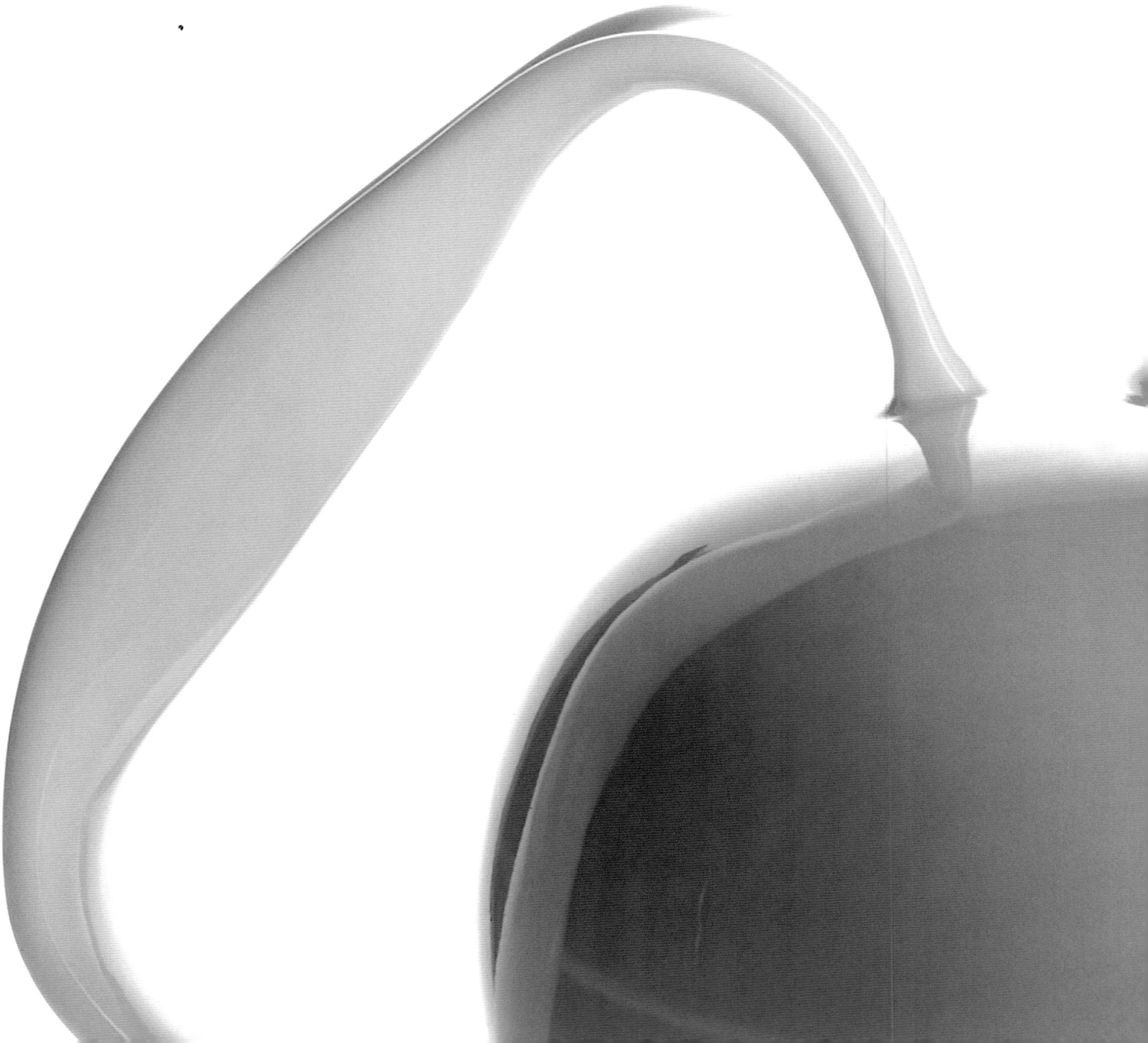

Fractal Modular Seating System

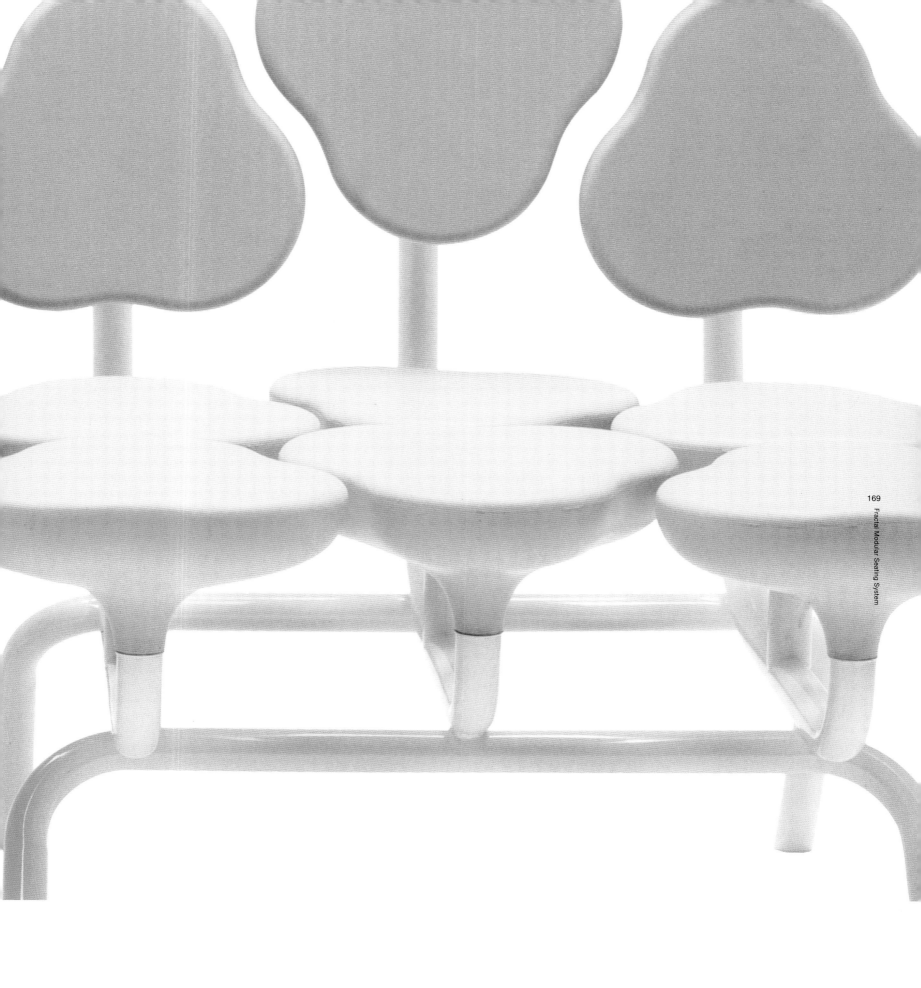

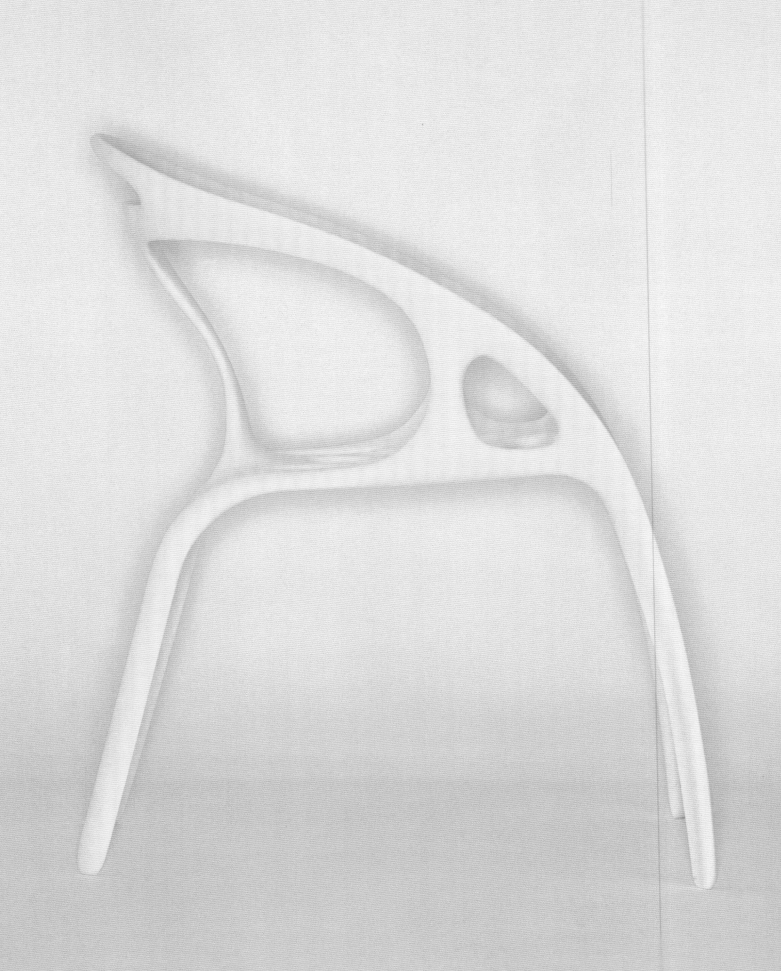

170

170
Gas Chair

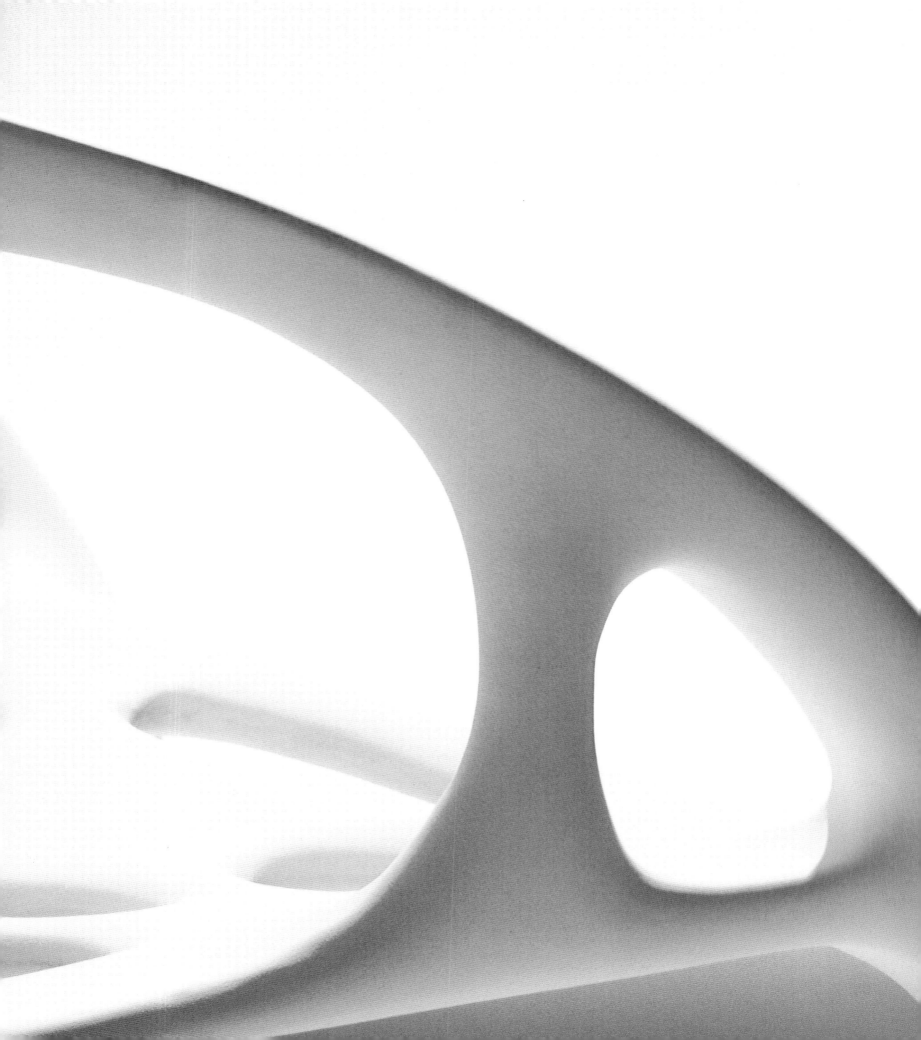

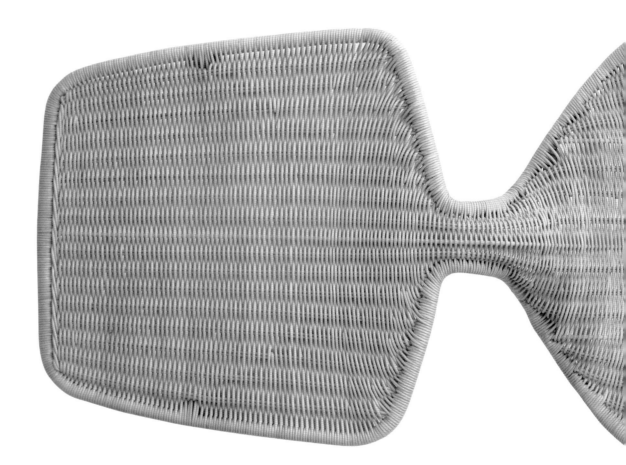

Apollo Rattan Lounger (Qwerty)

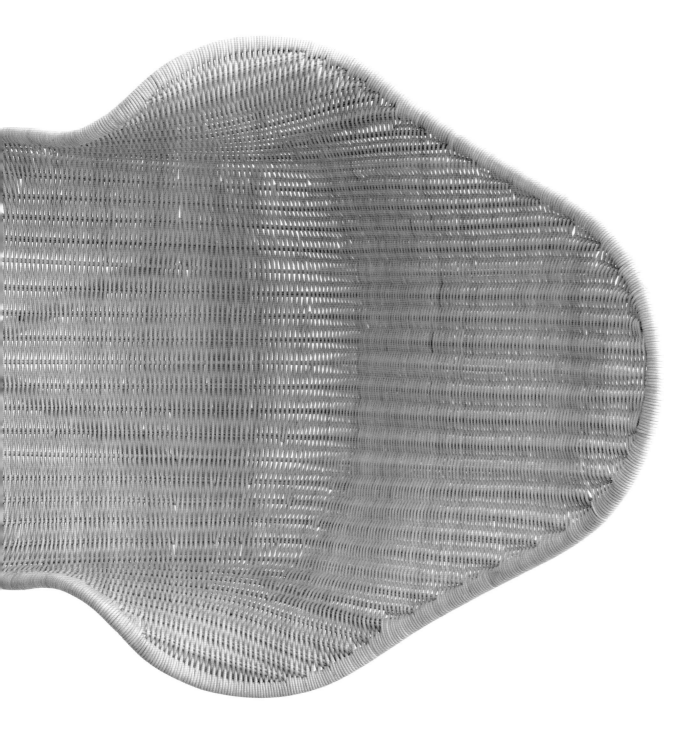

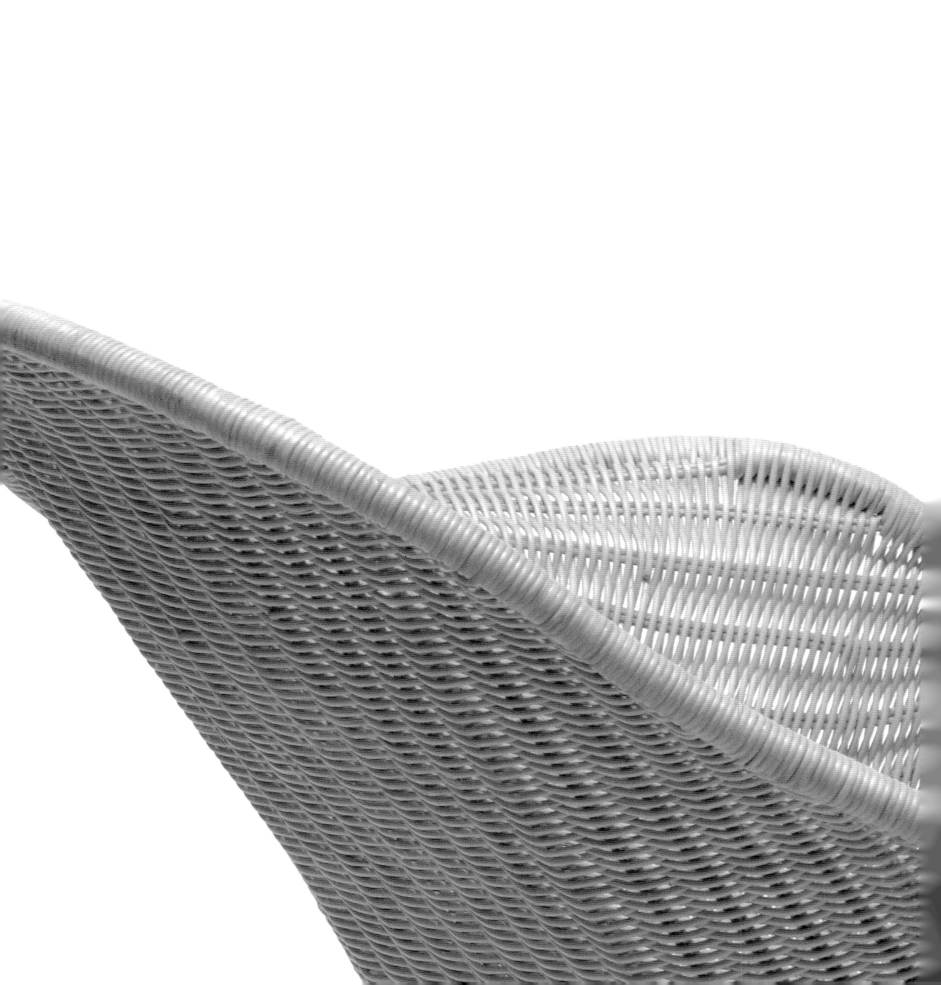

Apollo Rattan Lounger (Qwerty)

Spin (Geo) Chair

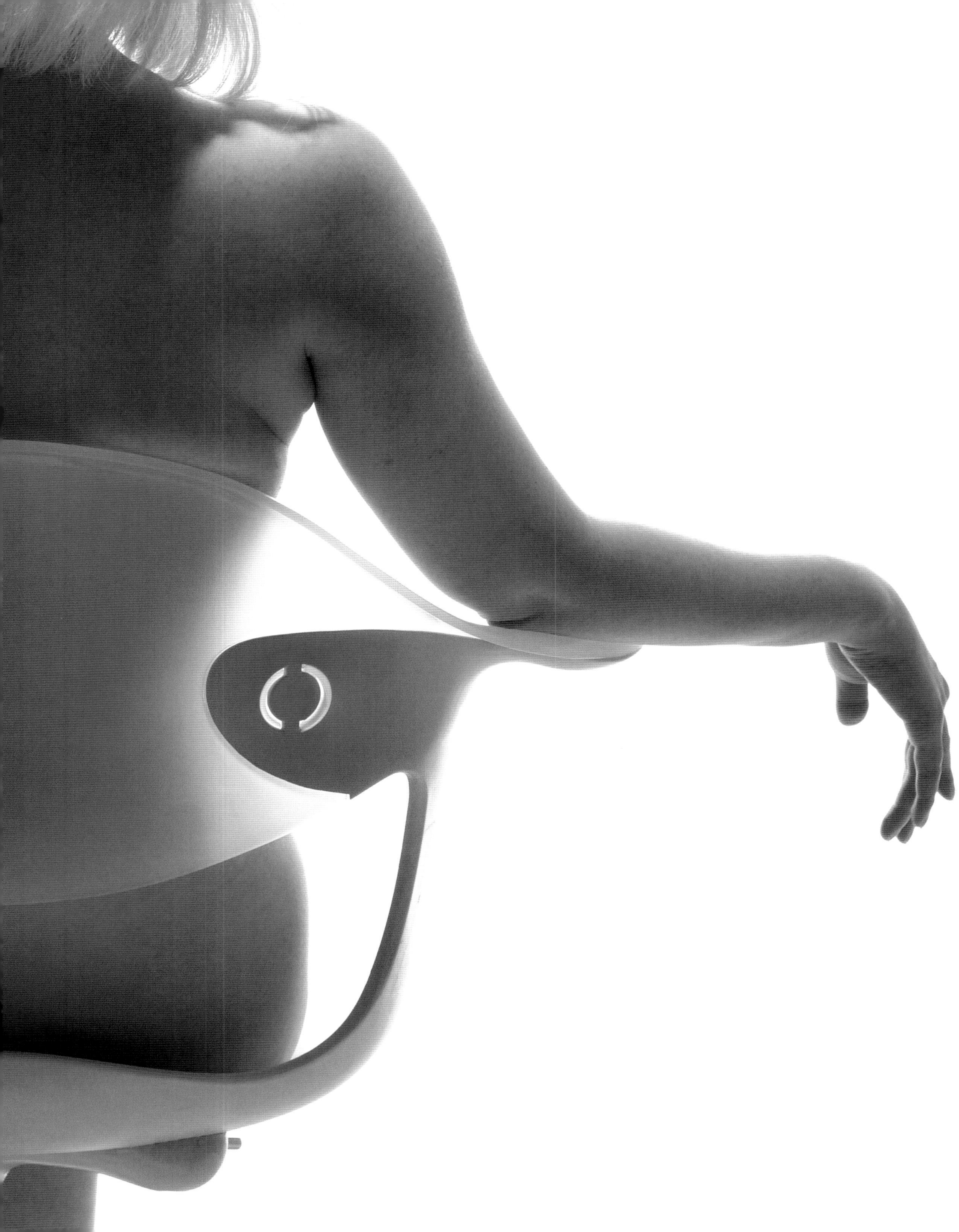

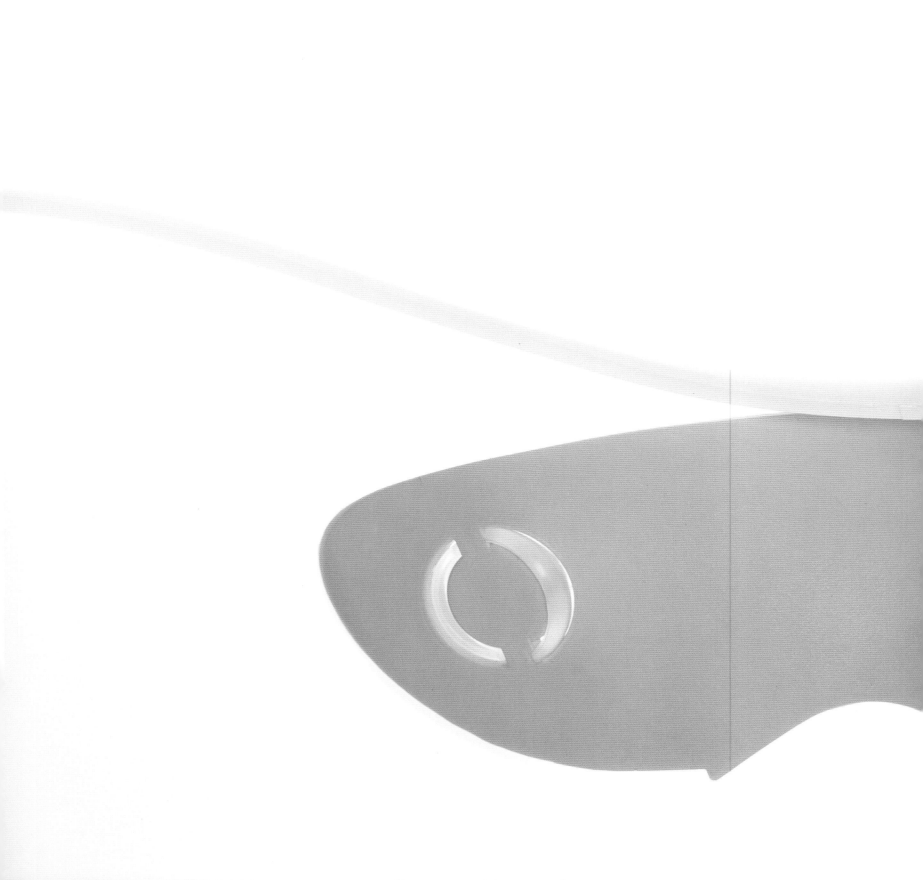

Aluminium Liquid Bench

Aluminium Liquid Tables

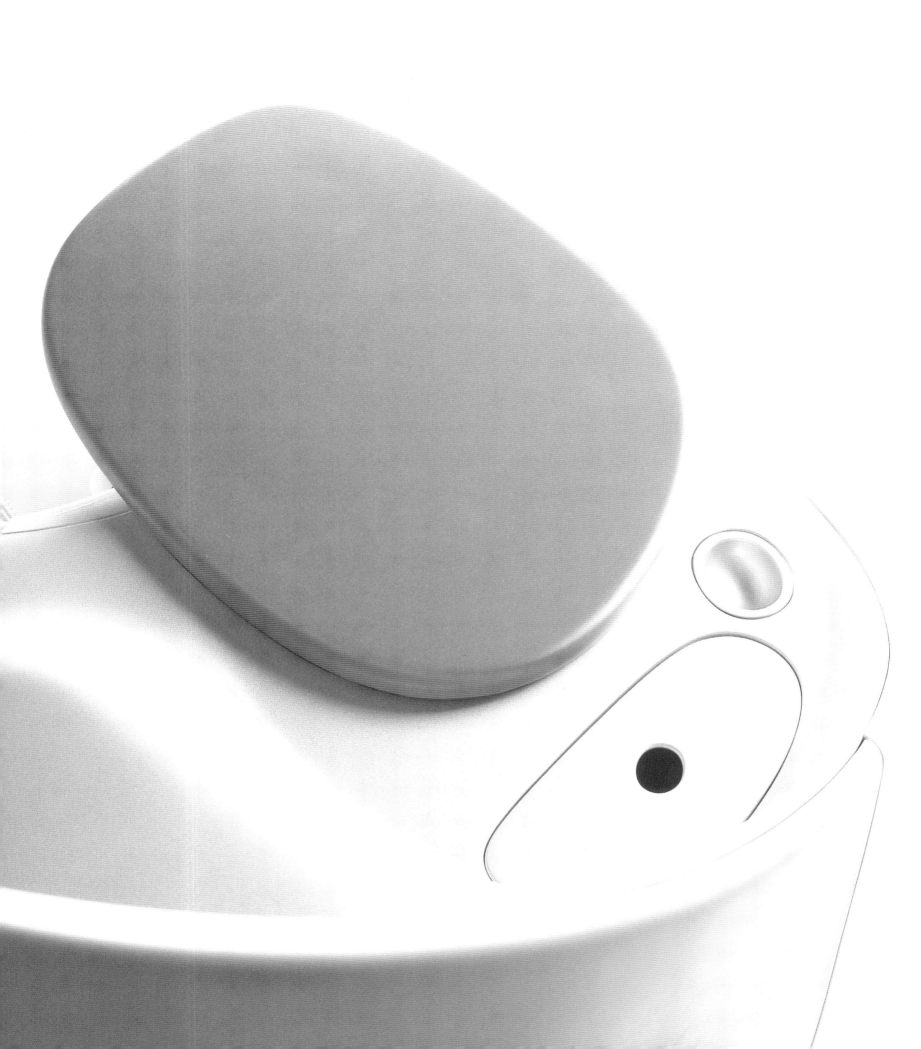

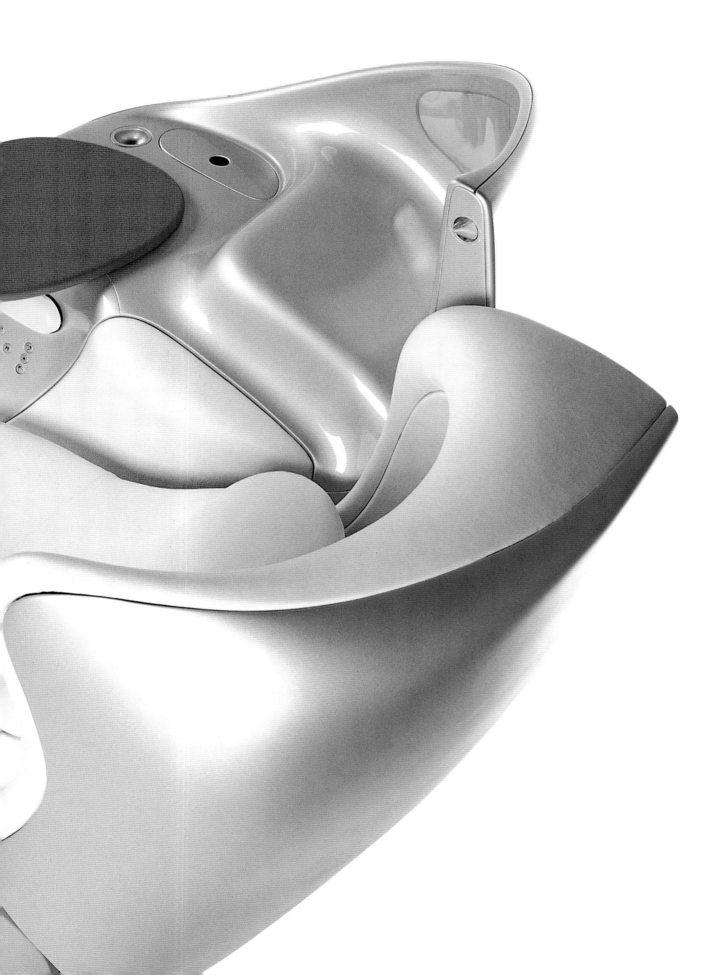

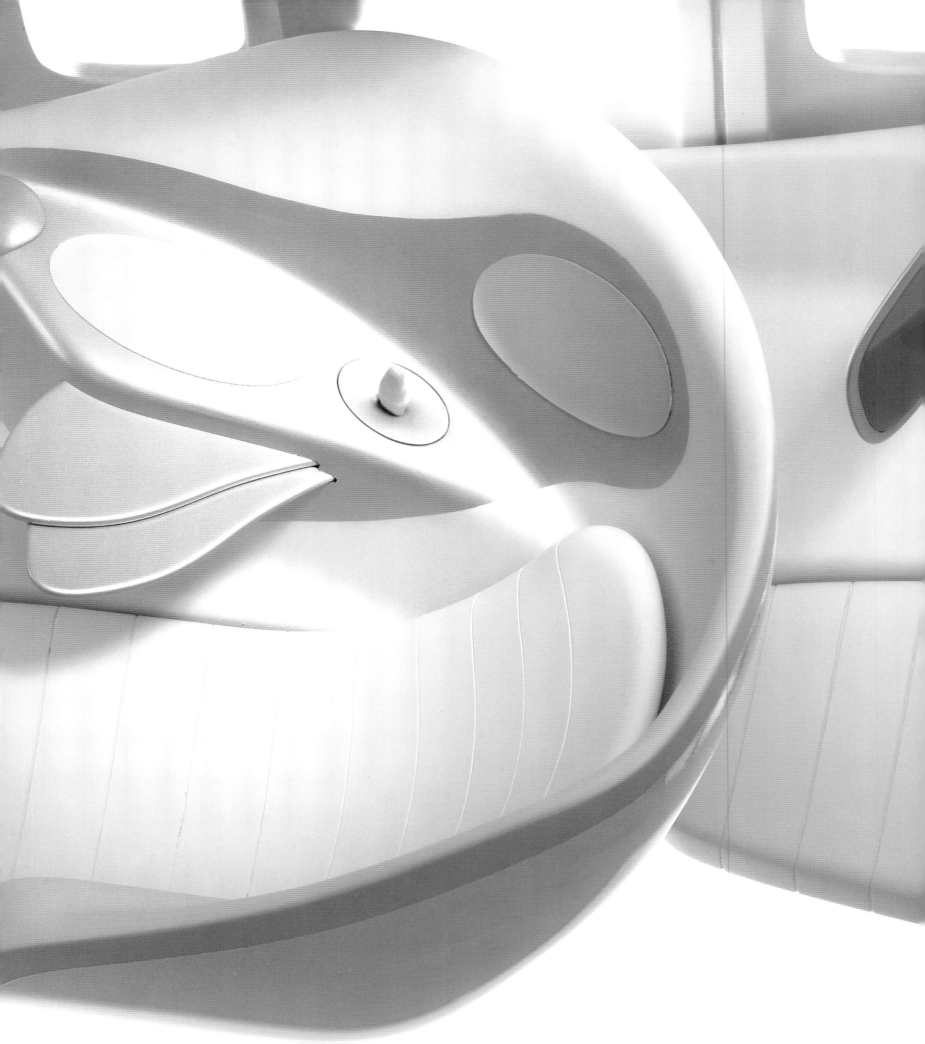

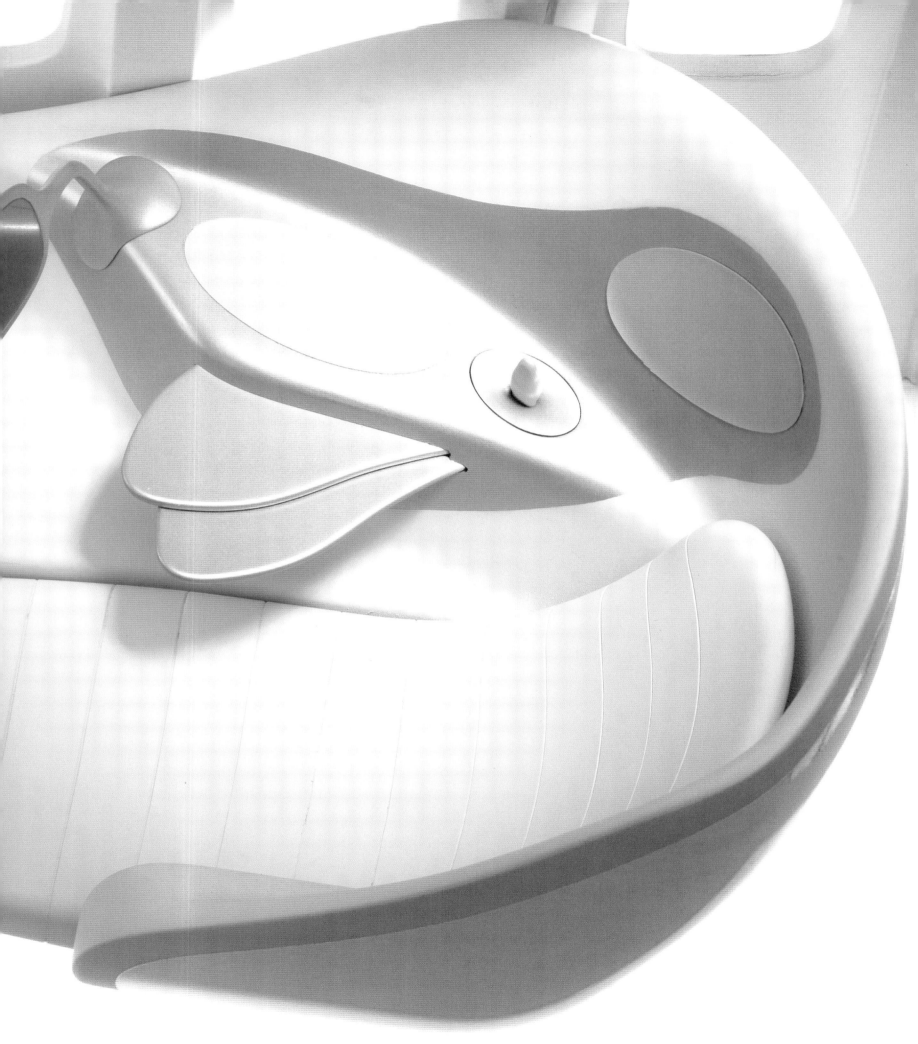

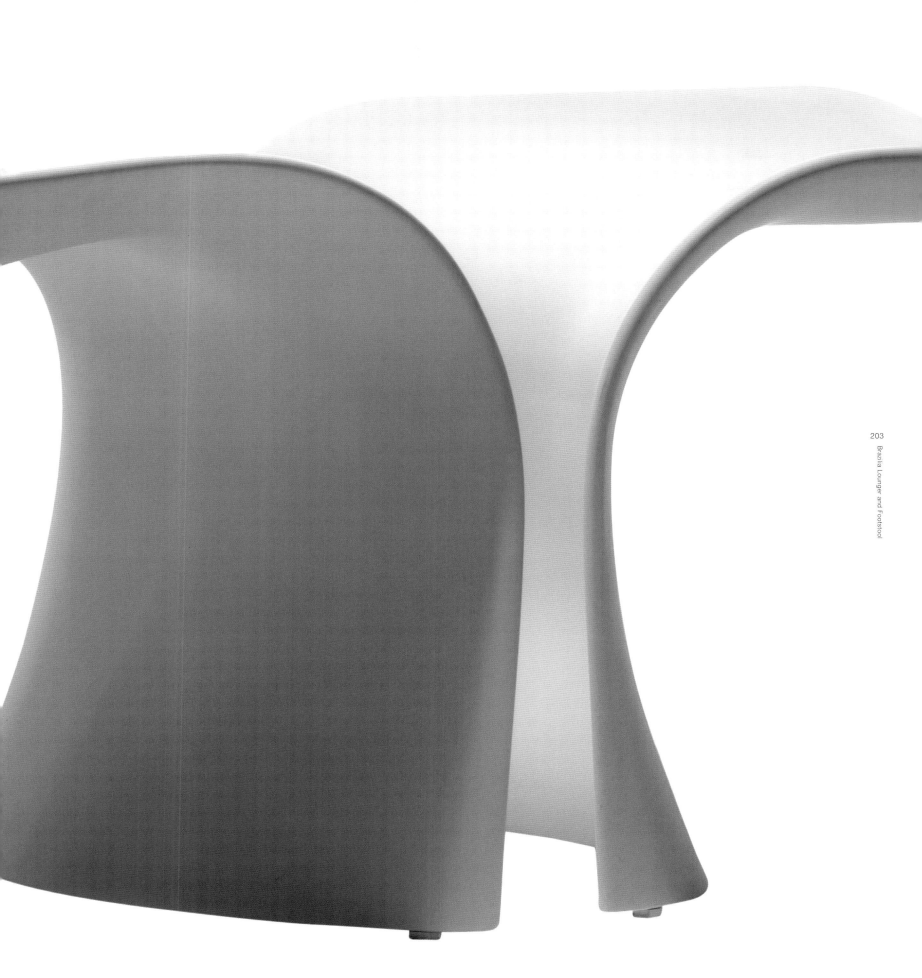

Optima Forma by Adriaan Beukers

Every time that designers confront me with their composite-material product ideas I wonder why they opt for fibre-reinforced plastic, especially when there is no need for lightness or durability. Is it the manifest form, the design possibilities offered, or is it that composite materials have a cool, trendy and innovative image today? These are the first questions that enter my mind when looking at the latest carbon fibre-reinforced designs for polymer chairs, tables and even perfume bottles.

How different was my reaction when I saw Ross Lovegrove's DNA Staircase – it was love at first sight and I became totally absorbed, not only because of its aesthetic beauty but also because it embodies progressive biomimetic properties.

What intrigued me was the design of the basic module, an organic blade, containing most of the essential elements, including an internal handrail, adding much structural integrity to the piece. The dimension of this blade appears perfect in terms of the equal distribution of strength and stiffness. This is an example of a match made in heaven between functionalism and mechanics resulting in a timeless beauty that is incomparable; Lovegrove has realized in this staircase a masterpiece with respect to sustainable production in composite fibres.

Avoiding time- and energy-consuming logistics to transform traditional materials from ore to raw materials, intermediates, and then final assembly into a product, Lovegrove has designed a stair module that can be produced in a very efficient timescale, after combining the right fibres, inserts and resin (the ingredients) in a mould; then applying pressure and heat to cure the blade expediently (the cooking). This is what we call downstream manufacturing in 'optima forma', when all unnecessary stages in a classic production cycle are eliminated and at the end the assembly becomes the responsibility of the consumer through intuitive systems logic.

An unexpected advantage of the material and technology chosen is the potential to incorporate smart applications by adding appropriate glass and metallic fibres. These elements are capable of making the staircase a sensor of signals or data, able to receive, to transmit or to damp sound and even to become an electric heat radiator. It is a technological catalyst for new ways of integrating new physical principles within architecture … a form of passive seducer, as I see it, that can enrich space with a new physical dimension that is functionally inspiring … not bad for an industrial product!

'The incorporation of random play and a margin of
underdetermined, uncontrolled investment are now seen to be
necessary ingredients of any strategy aimed at innovation...'

'...A decoded architecture – made strange – offers itself to inhabitation as an aleatoric field, anticipating and actively prefacing its own detournement.'[15]
Zaha Hadid and Patrick Schumacher

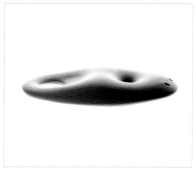

Ty Nant Waterbottle
Ty Nant, Wales, UK
1999–2001

Made from the same material and manufacturing technology as most high-volume mineral water bottles, this packaging product set out to communicate the universal importance and value of pure spring water by its intrinsic form and optical beauty.

pp12–27

Eye Digital Camera
Study
1992

This concept study of an elastomeric digital camera, proposed to the Olympus Optical Company in Japan, was the result of Lovegrove's research into the moulding of hydro-dynamic elastomeric materials and their use in biomorphic body-form structures for consumer products.

This proposal was intended to stimulate a radical new generation of products that would be non-precious, non-mechanical, soft and sensual – more akin to prosthetics than traditional products. As an extension of the body, the way in which a camera is used would become more bio-anatomical, tapping into a sense of self-containment and the nomadic.

pp30–35

Air One Low Armchair
Edra, Italy
1999

Air One is an appropriation of the materials and processes used in the disposable packaging of televisions, computers and white goods, resulting in the production of an armchair that is strong, impermeable, stackable, super-lightweight and recyclable.

It was made from expanded polypropylene beaded foam, a process Lovegrove first used in 1990 on the Surf computer accessories for Knoll, and later when designing lightweight portable screening for Herman Miller. With this chair he defines a new, innovative approach towards products and the impact they have on our environment. Air One is a manifestation of one of Lovegrove's defining credos, namely to extract physical usefulness from technological observation.

pp36–43

Basic Thermos Flask
In collaboration with Julian Brown
Alfi, Germany
1988–90

This product was the first successful commercial icon to demonstrate the beauty of transparency in everyday affordable products. Composed of a crystal-clear polycarbonate skin and a vacuum metallized inner glass flask, its design carried with it something of a new value system. This very functional object influenced many subsequent generations of products.

pp44–49

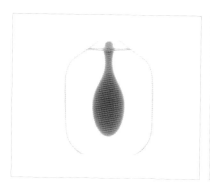   

Armani Perfume Bottle
Giorgio Armani/BPI, France
1992

This product is designed to be slim and portable. It is made from a unique combination of an inner glass flask that contains the perfume and a second form filled with a pocket of air that provides protection.

It was proposed that a further product could be made with eau de toilette replacing the air in the second cavity, as a compact travel solution for this type of product.

pp50–51

Bone Chair
Ceccotti, Italy
1994

This chair, made from sycamore wood as a one-off, is a sculptural exercise in the fluid reduction of structural form. The seat is made from carbon fibre that is bonded directly onto the wood section fusing the two fibrous materials together. The addition of the composite material does not affect the lightness of the piece, which has the feel of a lightweight sporting bow or an artefact from African tribal culture.

pp52–55

Biolove Aluminium Bicycle
Biomega, Denmark
1997–9

This bicycle frame is made by the process of superforming an aluminium sheet, trimmed into three components and subsequently bonded together to make a stiff and lightweight one-piece monocoque structure.

Its form is derived from that of a wishbone, linking all the necessary components of the steering and drive systems in the most direct and economical way possible.

The hole is there to lighten the bike's mass and to provide a detail from which to hang the bicycle on the wall, thereby saving space in restricted urban interiors.

pp58–63

Public Seating
bdlove.com, Spain
2000–3

Generous public seating units bring the joy of sculptural plastic forms to urbanized spaces.

They are made from roto-moulded polyethylene in a great variety of 'polymer' colours and are virtually indestructible, being resilient to shock, acids and ultraviolet light. Their geometry facilitates stacking and efficient transportation of the various pieces: a bench, a planter and a seating unit with an integrated lighting mast.

pp66–69

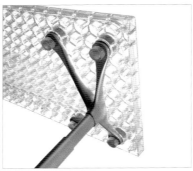

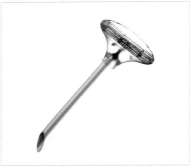

Public Seating
bdlove.com, Spain
2000–3

This series consists of three elements:
a bench, a planter and a lamp/seat.

All these elements are roto-moulded in
polyethylene, a process used
predominantly in the manufacture of
chemical containers.

The process has been perfected to
create the world's largest industrial-
scale seating unit for outdoor spaces.
The design of all three pieces
considers to the full all the benefits of
the material and its processing to
achieve products that are
indestructible, stackable for
transportation, colourful and
affordable.

The intention was to bring the
sculptural joy of polymer to the
domain of public spaces at maximum
scale relating to the walking man.

pp70–73

Office Furniture
Herman Miller, USA
In collaboration with Stephen Peart
1995–2000

The application of transparency and
the use of polymers to facilitate
modularity, lightness and economy
mark this project out in the field of
office design. This emphasis brings
with it a paradigm shift in the
perceived physical experience of the
new digital-material office.

Its minimum-inventory/maximum-
diversity set-up consists of a raised
floor system allowing the transfer of
power, data and other services
through a building, as well as
providing the structural integrity
required to permit the plugging-in of
legs and subsequent connection of
work surfaces and other ancillary
furniture. The result is a flexible and
highly adaptable solution for
emerging technologies and interactive
communication.

pp76–89

Solar Bud Outdoor Light
Luceplan, Italy
1995–8

The Solar Bud is the first product
ever to bear the inscription 'Made in
Europe'. It is also the first universal
commercial European lighting product
to use photovoltaic (solar) technology
for its energy source in combination
with high-efficiency LED. Its housing
is made from UV-resistant
polycarbonate, sealed by ultrasonic
welding to ensure the unit is
watertight and mounted on an
aluminium tube that contains a nickel
cadmium long-life battery.

Solar Bud is a statement of intent,
bringing awareness of ecological
design considerations to the
international communities of
architecture and design.

pp92–99

Angel Floor Lamp
Luceplan, Italy
2001–4

Two polycarbonate prismatic bubbles
on a steel stem provide two distinct
levels of light.

The lower level is at sitting height,
providing light for reading in bed or
next to a sofa. The higher-level bubble
brings light to the whole room,
providing light for dressing and
general atmospheric effect.

Both are adjusted by touch-sensitive
rings that can be accessed from any
orientation – sitting or standing.

pp100–101

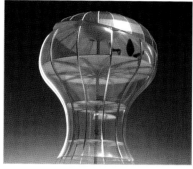

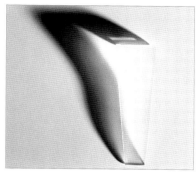

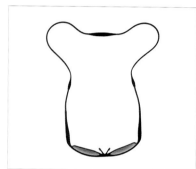

Agaricon Table Light
Luceplan, Italy
1999–2002

Somewhat resembling a mushroom, this injection-moulded polycarbonate light has a touch-sensitive circuit housed around the entire circumference of the elevated structure in an aluminium ring. Being circular and touch-sensitive, the light can be switched on, off or dimmed at will from any point about its 360-degree radius.

pp102–103

Solar Seed Nomadic Architecture
Solar power applications study
1994–onwards

The Solar Seed is a lightweight portable set of parts made from advanced materials and designed to be assembled into a new form of housing that is more akin to product than it is to architecture.

The seeds are intended for multiple purchase as autonomous structures that can be placed in the landscape. They are fuelled by solar canopies that rotate to track the sun, absorbing its energy with maximum efficiency.

pp104–105

Ceramic-bladed Razor
Techtonica, UK
1990–7

A specialized team was formed in the UK to develop this product which was made from high alumina, yttria zirconia ceramic lasting up to twenty-five times longer that a traditional inox-bladed razor.

Every year in the US alone 3 billion razors are consigned to the landfill, and it was the intention of this product to offer a sustainable alternative made possible by advances in ceramic powder development at a molecular level.

pp106–107

Physics Sunglasses
Tag Heuer, Switzerland
1997–onwards

Physics is a complete range of eyewear that uses high-technology materials and manufacturing principles in keeping with the company's position as a leading innovator in the field of high-precision timepieces and chronometers.

Made from an alloy of magnesium, titanium and aluminium the frames are lightweight, highly resilient and display subtle organic forms, providing an exacting level of performance and anatomical comfort.

As the company globally distributes the sunglasses to countries with people of different ethnic origin and facial features, a special patented nose bridge has been engineered to adapt to the different contours of the face.

pp108–109

Ammonite Palmtop Communicator
Apple Computer Corporation, USA
1994

Based on the Newton, the world's first intuitive palmtop, the Ammonite project explored the full potential of such software, looking at the integration of a cellular phone in relation to this compact technology. The form is derived from ergonomic principles and from the study of active and passive states of technology.

pp110–111

Disc Camera
Royal College of Art study project
1981–3

This is a response to the Kodak Disc – a camera innovation that used a micro-format rotational film system.

Through study and perseverance, the body-weight of the camera was reduced to that of a Coke can, eliminating in the process all superfluous detail. The film was necessarily repackaged into a ring-pull cassette that sat on, rather than within, the body of the product. This made the design slim and tactile; its outward material composition expressed the technological aesthetic of its innovation whilst retaining reference to its photographic origins. The camera won the 'Oggetti per Domus' award in 1984.

pp112–113

Loom Chaise Longue
Loom, Germany
1997–2000

The loom is a composite of paper wound tightly around a stainless steel wire core.

The technique was first developed in the 1920s as an economical alternative to rattan when making informal affordable domestic furniture.

Up until this project the loom had been nailed to a wooden subframe by hand. This new industrialized approach captures the material in an extruded aluminium frame to create a variety of seating typologies that are lightweight membranes: thin, strong and elegant.

pp114–115

Orbit Plywood Chair (Flyply)
Bernhardt Design, USA
2003

This chair is an advanced construction developed in Denmark that pushes the plywood and its forming to the limit. A 5mm shell thickness is achieved, giving the chair a perceived lightness. This is made possible by a double sandwich that is stiffened by the form of its inner cavity. This arrangement forms a blended spine that elegantly distributes structural support only where it is required.

pp116–119

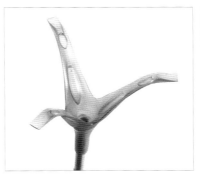

Villa Matoso
Donaca Ceramics, Portugal
1998–2000

Commissioned by Donaca Ceramics, a company with shared interests in the use of ceramics in new systems architecture, Villa Matoso was designed to function both as a private villa and as a visitors' centre.

Situated directly on the coastline, the structure was intended to be a construct employing extruded-tube technology to suggest an apparent metamorphosis in its physicality. The villa 'grows' outwards from aluminium tubing through to ceramic, milky polycarbonate, and finally emerges in transparent polycarbonate and glass as its aperture opens up to the light of the ocean.

pp120–125

Lugg Bicycle System
Biomega, Denmark
1997–2001

Tubes of different materials – from steel and aluminium to composites and polymer pultrusions – are connected by a system of forged joints, forming a traditional geometry with a new aesthetic rationale. The system is highly flexible and economical as the components are bonded together with a unique adhesive called Permabond ESP 110.

The bamboo version in this family was prototyped to demonstrate the full flexibility of the tube system and the potential use of organic sustainable materials.

All bicycles are fitted with a unique patented folding handlebar system, designed and developed by Ross Lovegrove, that allows them to be hung flush on the wall, saving space in urban situations.

pp126–135

Plantable Table Leg
Conceptual manufacturing
1998

This is a proposal for a table leg that is grown in a bamboo plantation. It is achieved when a biopolymer connector is placed onto a shoot which then extends vertically, fusing the two materials together to form a product.

The leg is cultivated and dipped in natural rubber to form a foot. It was conceived for the 1998 exhibition 'Patas' in Valencia.

pp138–139

Go Chair
Bernhardt Design, USA
1998–2001

This chair, manufactured from pressure die-cast magnesium, is the first of its kind in terms of its use of such technology, material and fluid organic language in the field of furniture design.

Seen as defining a new aesthetic for the twenty-first century, born out of an anatomical approach to form and produced in light of the advanced principles of automative precision manufacturing, the Go Chair was selected by *Time Magazine* as one of the finest examples of design in the year 2001. Recently chosen by Tadao Ando for his new Fort Worth Museum of Contemporary Art in Texas, it is actively collected by various museums around the world.

pp140–147

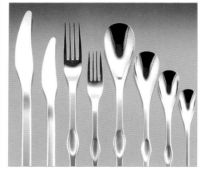

Biowood Sculpture
Ceccotti, Italy
1999

These pieces follow on from research into the subconscious nature of the creation of form.

They describe space and growth whilst simultaneously exploring fluidity, liquidity and the possibility to evolve sculptural forms that are between the natural and artificial worlds that we know. The data of the mind in its randomness is transferred into three dimensions without need for validation with purpose or functionality.

pp150–155

Torch
rosslovegrove.com, UK
2003–onwards

This is a product whose design is informed through the observation of its use. A subtle innovation gives rise to a unique iconographic shape made memorable by the nature of this form and the gesture it clearly represents: a beam facing forward and a beam facing downward to illuminate the user's path.

Recharged on its own special plinth, the torch functions as a bedside light for the majority of its life.

pp156–157

Solo Stainless Steel Cutlery
Driade, Italy
1996

This collection explores the nature of stainless steel in relation to the forging process. It does this to arrive at a balance in the hand assisted by a gentle point of registration in the handle related to the formality or informality of use.

The shape of the spoon heads are not new as they are derived and adapted from spoons studied at the British Museum from the fifteenth century, a time when spoons were regarded as one of the most important tools in daily use and therefore highly developed in terms of beauty and functionalism.

pp158–159

Hackman Tools Cookware Collection
Hackman Designor, Finland
1996–2000

Advanced technopolymer and stainless steel.

This full collection of industrialized cookware, along with a plywood serving trolley, is the first to break free from the standard industrial code of black thermoset polymer in this area of product design.

Created out of a spirit of advanced technology, and its potential to injection-mould glass with white technopolymer, the tools demonstrate a sense of beauty and relevance in material combination, very much in keeping with Scandinavian tradition and its refined value system.

This collection and its approach give a key insight into how the cultural and commercial significance of design can point a way forward for the future development of industries that have lain dormant through lack of technological innovation.

pp160–163

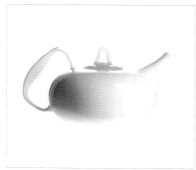

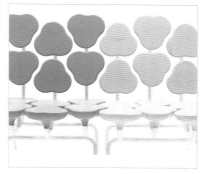

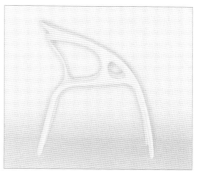

Ceramic Tea Cup
Driade, Italy
1996

The cup, with its handle flowing from its body, is an example of organic essentialism, since its unity of material and form are guided by its balanced ergonomic posture.

pp164–165

Ceramic Tea Pot
Driade, Italy
1996

The handle of this teapot is shaped and positioned to transfer the weight of the vessel in use through to the anatomical form of the hand so that it feels stiff and satisfyingly secure. The silicone lid takes up the tolerance of the ceramic and so does not rattle or threaten to fall out during pouring.

pp166–167

Fractal Modular Seating System
IDEE Corporation, Japan
1995

Designed for an exhibition at IDEE in Tokyo in 1995, the pieces consisted of a bench, an upright chair, a snaking bench, stools, bar tables and high stools.

The pieces were made with low investment in Pisa and Tokyo and were never commercialized.

They were made in a multiple of three in three separate colours, grey, yellow and turquoise. A single bench is now in Ross Lovegrove's studio in London, while the rest remain with Teruo Kurosaki at IDEE in Tokyo.

A set of Fractal collages mounted in specially designed frames were created to accompany the exhibition.

pp168–169

Gas Chair
Form application study
1998

This chair represents a study into the process of gas injection in relation to organic forms and perforated surfaces.

It is influenced by the way bones are reduced and lightened by negative cavities and holes. This chair therefore explores a new organic aesthetic that promotes 'sinuous mass' reduction in an attempt to find hidden essential forms that celebrate plasticity.

pp170–173

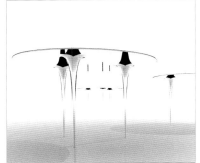

Apollo Rattan Lounger (Qwerty)
Driade, Italy
1996

Apollo represents a new furniture
typology that has been created by the
ergonomic adaptation of the seat's
usual function.

On a typical chaise longue it is
impossible to straddle the seat in
order to use the surface for other
functions – something that people
wish to do most instinctively.

The new shape has been derived from
a form of outline erosion that allows
the user a new freedom in the seat's
daily function, from lying and resting
to the use of the foot tablet for
reading, computer work or informal
eating.

It is lightweight, durable and therefore
non-precious, promoting regular use.

pp174–179

Spin (Geo) Chair
Driade, Italy
1997–8

The chair's two-piece shell exploits
the dual characteristics of the
polymer's inherent properties of
rigidity and flexibility, opacity and
translucency. It gently moves with the
body in use, creating a pleasing level
of support that is ergonomically
passive.

The form of the chair was developed
from the study of the way our mass
and weight interact with the rounded
surfaces that are required to obtain
structural integrity in the use of
single-skin polymers without ribbing.

It therefore adheres to established
modernist principles of ergonomic
geometry but the use of non-exotic
polymers makes the chair accessible,
economical and easy to disassemble
should recycling ever be required.

pp180–183

Aluminium Liquid Bench
Form application study
2002

With the Liquid Bench, Lovegrove
chose to explore the relationship
between essential structure, liquid
form and potential use of mono-
material technology.

pp184–187

Aluminium Liquid Tables
Cappellini, Italy
2002

The legs are made to feel as if they
have dripped, under their own weight
and viscosity, from the underside of
the tabletops.

pp188–189

Oasi Armchair and Footstool

Frighetto, Italy
1998

These are biomorphic forms that explore anatomic asymmetry in relation to the human body.

The Oasi Armchair uses a hidden internal steel frame to cantilever the back into free space so as to appear to defy gravity and support the sitter effortlessly. Its white leather surface is taut, achieving a sculptural appearance through its honed and purposeful skin.

pp190–191

Sky Sleeper Solo Aircraft Seat

Japan Airlines, Japan
1998–2001

The seat provides a new aesthetic approach to the creation of personal space on a commercial aircraft. Its full, three-dimensional form cocoons the passenger, creating a micro-environment that defines a high level of psychological and physiological comfort.

The seat is an anatomically sculpted assembly of hard and soft elements, the form of which has been arrived at by the study of interactive space as defined by the body in its upright, recumbent and fully reclined positions. The negative forms at the back of the seats are therefore derived from the interlocution of body forms and the need to arrive at an efficient cabin configuration that affords the passenger maximum ownership of space.

The seat won the Japan's 'G' Mark federal prize in 2002 and was exhibited at the Roosevelt Centre, New York, in 2003, to mark the 100th anniversary of the Wright brothers' first successful manned flight.

pp192–199

Brazilia Lounger and Footstool

Zanotta, Italy
2003

Manufactured in lacquered, cold-cure rigid polyurethane, this single undulating surface rises elegantly from the floor plane as if created by antigravity.

The pieces defy scale as sculptural elements that continue Lovegrove's exploration of fluid elastic forms in structural design.

pp200–203

DNA Staircase

rosslovegrove.com, UK
2003

The DNA Staircase bridges product design and architecture, demonstrating its designer's philosophy towards the coalition of beauty and logic, as inspired by natural forms.

Made using the process of bladder moulding – a contemporary technology developed in the field of high-performance, composite material component manufacture – DNA is the first project to be both designed and produced by Ross Lovegrove. It is made from a combination of fibreglass and unidirectional carbon, endowing the piece with enormous structural integrity and resilience. It achieves much through its minimalism with form, material and technology working in unison, not unlike the structure of bone; it is informed with evolutionary purpose.

pp204-213

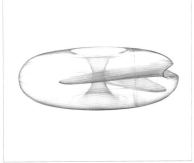

Ross Lovegrove Studio

rosslovegrove.com, UK
2003

Lovegrove's new studio in London is on two levels: one at ground and one at subterranean. The lower level, excavated to a depth of six metres provides the main studio area and is illuminated by a computerized daylight system that links both spaces and provides a natural condition of comfort. The system was especially developed for the studio by iGuzzini Illuminazione in Italy.

The space was designed by Miska Miller-Lovegrove whose work, being rational and modernist, provided clean linear volumes that are functionally elegant. The architect sourced a combination of unique materials and technologies from Japan and Germany, including honeycomb bubble polycarbonate work-surfaces and foam aluminium large four metre doors for the storage wall.

Alongside iGuzzini the sponsors of the studio included; Leitner, Germany, Beat Karrer, Switzerland, C2, Driade and Luceplan, Italy

pp214–215

Graz Conceptual Architecture

SLA Model at 1/200 scale,
rapid prototyping in resin
2003

The study of elastic surfaces frozen into habitable space where all is holistically integrated is as an expression of new organic essentialism and a drive towards a new physicality in architecture born out of technology transfer and speculative new forms of industrialization.

Frozen Elastic Architecture was shown as part of the 'Latent Utopias' exhibition curated by Zaha Hadid and Patrick Schumacher, an event that 'focused on current experiments with radically new concepts of space that are proliferating on the back of the new electronic design media today'.

pp216–219

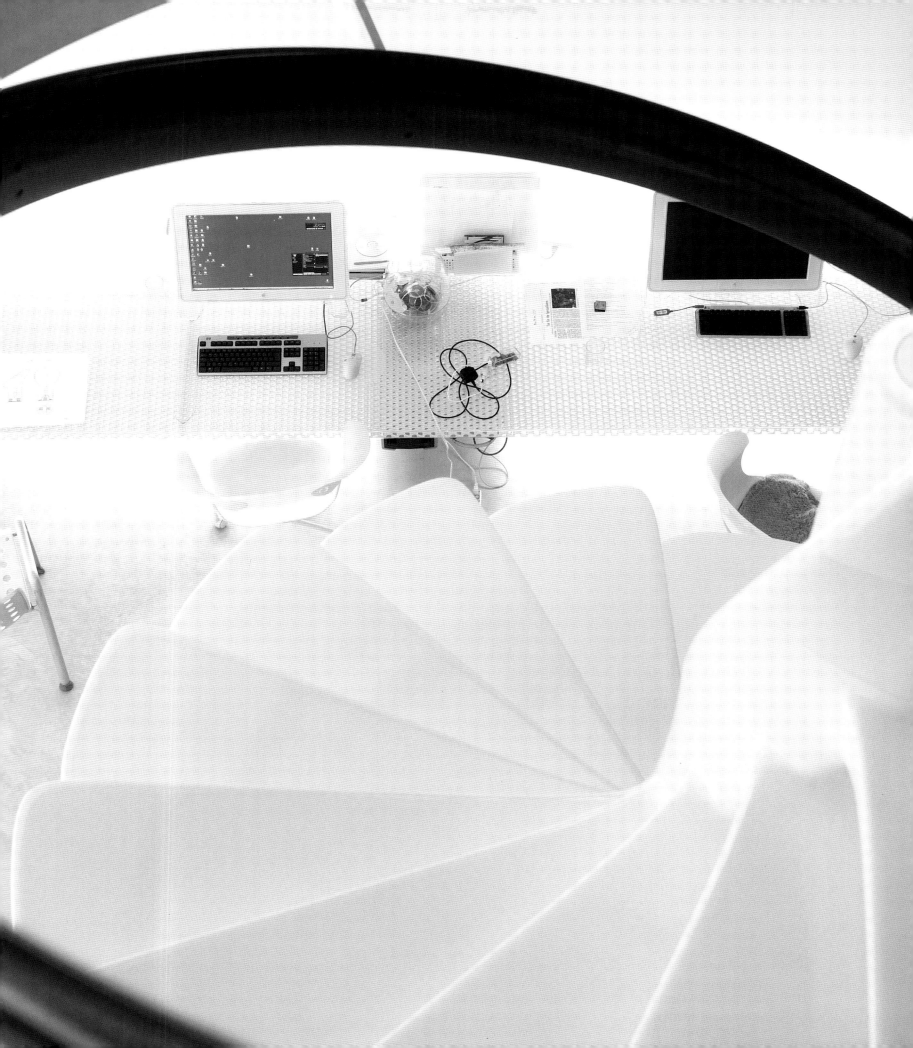

Notes

Selected Bibliography

1 Reyner Banham, *Los Angeles: The Architecture of Four Ecologies*, Icon (Harpe),1971

2 Paola Antonelli, *Objects of Design from The Museum of Modern Art*, The Museum of Modern Art, New York, 2003

3 Arthur Drexler and Eliot Noyes *Charles Eames Furniture from the Design Collection*, The Museum of Modern Art, New York, 1973

4 Isamu Noguchi, *Essays and Conversations*, Harry N Abrams in association with the Isamu Noguchi Foundation, 1994, p31, 'Towards a Reintegration of the Arts' (1949),

5 Adriaan Beukers & Ed Van Hinte *Lightness,* 010 Publishers, 1998, p25

6 Janine M Benyus*, Biomimicry, Innovation Inspired by Nature*, Perennial Harper Collins, 2002, p261

7 *ibid*, p243

8 Peter Pearce *Structure in Nature is a Strategy for Design*, MIT Press, 1978, ppxii–xiii

9 *ibid*, pxii

10 Alberto Meda, in correspondence with Ross Lovegrove

11 *ibid*

12 Janine M Benyus, *op cit*, p110

13 Peter Pearce, *op cit*, pxv

14 Isamu Noguchi, *op cit*, p35, 'Meanings in Modern Sculpture' (1949)

15 Zaha Hadid & Patrick Schumacher *Latent Utopias Experiments within Contemporary Architecture* Steirscher Herbst, 2002, p8

Alexandra Papadakis, *Innovation: from experimentation to realisation*, Andreas Papadakis, London/New York, 2003

Phil Patton, 'Going With The Flow: Tech Nouveau Arrives', *New York Times*, 6 November 2003

'Uno studio prototipo', *Domus*, 862, September 2003

'Design for living: Astro Lamp', *The Independent on Sunday*, 22 June 2003

'"Latente Utopien"/ "Enactments of the Self"', *Artforum International*, 1 February 2003

Ellen Lupton, *Skin: Surface, Substance and Design,* Princeton Architectural Press, New York, 2002

Ross Lovegrove (ed.), *The International Design Yearbook 2002*, Laurence King, London, 2002

Zaha Hadid & Patrick Schumacher, *Latent Utopias: Experiments within Contemporary Architecture,* Steirscher Herbst, New York, 2002

das weiten suchen – expanding the gap, Edition Axel Menges, London/ Stuttgart, 2002

'Furniture', *Interior Design*, 31 October 2002

Maria Helena Estrada, 'Ross Lovegrove Etica e Estética', *Arc Design*, 27, São Paulo, September/ October 2002

Sheila Kim, 'Serpentine logic', *Interior Design*, 1 August 2002

'Gimme Shelter', *The Independent*, 29 June 2002

'Cover Interview', *Axis,* vol 97, Tokyo, May/June 2002

'A designer with bottle', *The Independent*, 18 May 2002

'A Message in The Bottle?', *The Washington Post*, 5 April 2002

Ramón Ubeda, 'La aventura española de Ross Lovegrove', *Diseño Interior,* 122, 2002

Charlotte and Peter Fiell, 'Ross Lovegrove', in *Designing the twenty-first century*, Taschen, Cologne, 2001

'Design – The Best and Worst of 2001', *Time Magazine*, 24 December 2001

'Japan Airlines to use design by Ross Lovegrove in first-class cabin', *Axis,* vol 94, Tokyo, November/December 2001

'The 50 Best Ways To Light Up Your Life', *The Independent*, 20 October 2001

Franchesca Picchi, 'Organic Minimalism', *Domus*, 838, June 2001

Ivan Ezersky, 'Ross Lovegrove, Designer of the Year', NG-Koulisa, Moscow, 2 February 2001

'Liquid Solids', *Esquire*, March 2000

Peter Fiell, 'La nuova natura', *Domus*, 795, July 1997

Vanni Pasca, 'Ross Lovegrove: sensual organicity', *Driade Edizioni,* 4, April 1997

Vanni Pasca, 'Lighting affinities', *Luceplan*, Milan 1996

Juli Capella, 'In/Off, Salone del Mobile', *Domus*, 784, July 1996

'English Leather', *I.D. Magazine*, May/June 1996

'All you need is Lovegrove', *The Sunday Times Magazine*, 31 March 1996

'Design-High', *Wohn Design*, 3,

November/December 1995

'5,000 Türgriffe in einem Gebäude...' *Möbel Raum Design*, October/ November 1995

'Lovegrove', *Design Report*, 10, October 1995

'Old England discovers design', *Blueprint*, 117, May 1995

'A good hiding', *The Magazine*, 9 April 1995

'British Grace', *Form*, 1, 1995

Paola Antonelli, 'Mutant Materials in Contemporary Design', The Museum of Modern Art, New York, 1995

'Ross Lovegrove, designer', *Intramuros*, 56, December 1994

'Spazi High-touch', *Interni*, 445, November 1994

'Ross Lovegrove', *Domus*, 765, November 1994

'I "pensieri della mano" di Ross Lovegrove', *Interni*, 444, October 1994

'Una nuova fiducia scultorea', *Domus*, 758, March 1994

'Ross Lovegrove', *Galeries Magazine*, February/March 1994

'Clandestine Cool', *Marie Claire Japon*, 150, 1994

'The Conran Foundation', *Abitare*, 324, December 1993

Enrico Morteo, 'La qualitá della scrittura', *Domus*, 745, January 1993

Marco Romanelli, 'Figure of 8 chair', *Domus*, 743, November 1992

'In nuova forma', *Casa Vogue*, 24, September 1992

237

Acknowledgements

239

I would like to express my gratitude for all friends, family, staff and clients who have supported me over the years, without whose commitment a book like this would not have been possible. A heartfelt thank you to Emilia Terragni and Richard Schlagman of Phaidon Press for insisting on the highest quality of production for this work; Yumi Matote and John Ross, who together have produced artwork and photography that I find very beautiful and, above all, true to their own creative eyes.

I would also like to thank my friends Paola Antonelli, Tokujin Yoshioka, Greg Lynn, Dr Adriaan Beukers, Cecil Balmond and Alberto Meda, whose work I very much respect and whose essays help me to understand my own work, inspiring a renewed vision in my thoughts for the future. Lastly and most importantly I would like to dedicate this first book to Miska and Roman who are always there at the core of my creative world to support my organic dreams.

Ross Lovegrove

240   Phaidon Press Limited
Regent's Wharf
All Saints Street
London N1 9PA

Phaidon Press Inc
180 Varick St, 14th Floor
New York NY 10014

www.phaidon.com

First published 2004
© 2004 Phaidon Press Limited

ISBN 0 7148 4367 9

Designed by Yumi Matote
Printed in China

All photographs by John Ross
except: p79 Patrick Gries, from The
Hand of Nature: Collection Anne &
Jacques Kerchache, Fondation
Cartier pour l'art contemporain, Paris,
2000; pp67–8, 69 bottom, 70 Estudicolor,
pp74–5,136–7 Ross Lovegrove; pp192–5
Lee Funnell; computer renderings: front cover,
pp18, 20–1, 68–73, 156–7, 184–9, 208, 218–9
Tim Williamson; pp60–1 Sebastian
Liedtk.